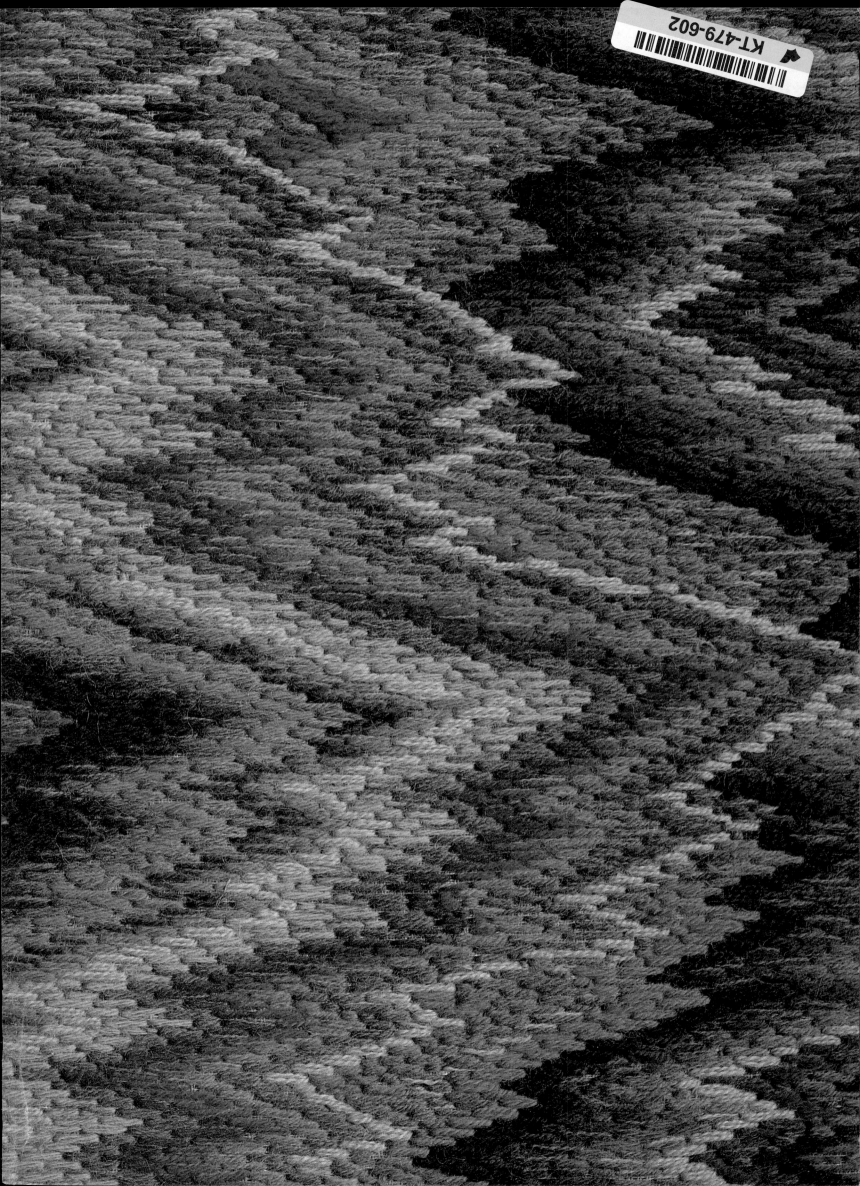

KAFFE FASSETT

GLORIOUS NEEDLEPOINT

PHOTOGRAPHY BY STEVE LOVI

To Sue B.
with love for your 1988 Birthday,
'Brett'

KAFFE FASSETT
GLORIOUS NEEDLEPOINT
PHOTOGRAPHY BY STEVE LOVI

CENTURY

London ▪ Melbourne ▪ Auckland ▪ Johannesburg

This book is dedicated to my mother and all the other teachers
in my life who opened my eyes to colour and pattern.

Editor/Sally Harding
Design/Cherriwyn Magill
Charts/Colin Salmon and Clare Clements
Illustrations/Sally Holmes

First published in 1987 by Century Hutchinson Ltd,
Brookmount House, 62–65 Chandos Place, Covent Garden,
London WC2N 4NW

Century Hutchinson Australia Pty Ltd,
PO Box 496, 16–22 Church Street, Hawthorn, Victoria 3122,
Australia

Century Hutchinson New Zealand Ltd,
PO Box 40-086, Glenfield, Auckland 10,
New Zealand

Century Hutchinson South Africa Pty Ltd,
PO Box 337, Bergvlei, 2012 South Africa
Reprinted 1987
British Library Cataloguing in Publication Data

Fassett, Kaffe
Glorious needlepoint: over 20 exclusive
designs.
1. Canvas embroidery
I. Title   II. Lovi, Steve
746.44′2   TT778.C3

ISBN 0 7126 1693 4

Phototypeset by Tradespools Ltd, Frome, Somerset
Colour origination by Alpha Reprographics Ltd,
Perivale
Printed in Spain by
Printer industria gráfica s.a. Barcelona
D.L.B. 18088-1987

(Title page and opposite title page)
Girl and boy needlepoint cushions
(see pages 106–109)

CONTENTS

INTRODUCTION
6

FRUITS AND VEGETABLES
12

FISH AND FOWL
32

FLOWERS AND FOLIAGE
54

FACES AND FANS
88

JUGS AND GEOMETRICS
118

EHRMAN KITS
150

NEEDLEPOINT TECHNIQUES
152

ACKNOWLEDGEMENTS
158

YARN AND KIT INFORMATION
158

INDEX
160

INTRODUCTION

KNITTING hooked me in its mysterious web when I first arrived in England in the mid-Sixties. Shortly after commencing that love affair which eventually led to my first book, *Glorious Knitting*, I was introduced to my second passion – needlepoint. These two obsessions have kept me happily absorbed for over twenty years.

The beauty of needlepoint is that the actual technique is even easier to learn than basic knitting. Before attempting needlepoint, I had the idea that it required a daunting amount of patience to produce. Imagine my amazement and delight when my first attempt at stitching flowed along so effortlessly that I was done in no time. I have taught many people to stitch on canvas in a matter of minutes. Some have even gone on to work on important commissions for me within an hour of learning. So, armed with this wonderful craft and astounding ranges of coloured wools, the world is your oyster!

This book is a peek into my creative process – dealing particularly with the translation of easily found source material into needlepoint. I intend to infuse you with the confidence to produce your own colour schemes and designs. By demystifying the act of designing, I hope I can help you to enjoy the childlike pleasure of playing with my favourite themes.

DISCOVERING NEEDLEPOINT

My own story in needlepoint design should indicate how simple designing can be. When Lady Harlech, then working for *Vogue* magazine, saw my first knitted garments, she asked me to draw a design for a pair of needlepoint slippers. As I designed, I began to wonder how difficult the stitching would be. Very, I concluded, observing

the neat rows of tent stitches on the finished slippers.

Lady Harlech was delighted with the end results and asked me to design a cushion for her. I painted the outlines of a glass paperweight in acrylics onto a 10-mesh canvas. The circles of repeated motifs made a flower-like pattern that looked fun to stitch. After watching a friend doing tent stitch, I filled in a few colours on my design to see the effect, and before I knew it I had completed the entire cushion. Astounded

■ *(Right) Matching the subtle colours to the woven tapestry backdrop, for my garden tapestry bench needlepoint.*

■ *(Far right) I designed the Harlech slippers before I had done any actual stitching. I would use more colours and shading if re-doing them today.*

6

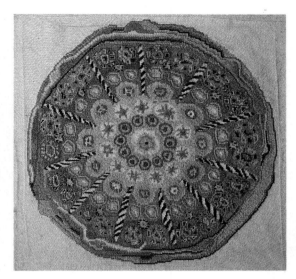

and totally turned on, I rushed out to buy more canvas and yarn to try other ideas. The mosaic plate (page 111) followed. To achieve the detail I wanted, I chose a fine canvas, but because of the fine yarn and tiny tent stitches it took months to complete and I nearly threw in the sponge. After that experience, I tried the quicker random long stitch (see page 153) for a workshop project involving several friends, and the Cosmos tapestry (page 139) was born.

COSMOS AND HERITAGE TAPESTRIES

The Cosmos tapestry sowed a seed in my mind. Eleven friends, most of whom had never attempted any creative work before, stitched beautiful harmonies of colour. I

realized that most people have a personal sense of colour and form which is released with a little confidence. There are many things that erode this confidence – over-

analyzing, for instance. It is best to plunge in and surprise yourself at the beauty, wit and harmony you can produce. The Heritage tapestry (details on page 101) is further proof of this.

Remembering the success of the Cosmos tapestry, I had the brainwave to create a huge, positive statement to combat the gloom of Britain in the early Eighties. I arranged to appear on the BBC's *Pebble Mill at One* television programme, where I demonstrated how to do a picture in tent

stitch on a 15cm/6″ square of canvas. I then asked all and sundry to send me a colourful needlepoint picture of anything the stitcher wanted to celebrate. The sub-title of this proposed Heritage tapestry was 'Count Your Blessings'. In the next two months 2,500 pieces of needlepoint flowed through my letterbox! I was moved to tears at the inventive, delicious portraits of gardens, children, animals, streets, houses, cars and boats. Many of the men, women and children who contributed, from every corner of Britain, stated with amazement that they had never attempted anything creative before and were now going on to do more decorative work. Student helpers and I then put a border of grey blocks around each picture and sewed them into 2.5m/8ft by 60cm/2ft panels of a fourteen-panel screen. Julia Lewandowskyj (then a Liverpool Polytechnic art student) spent all summer laboriously sewing the panels together, and

(Far left above) This paperweight is my first attempt at stitching. Repeating patterns make good projects to begin with.

(Far left) As the thousands of little needlepoint pictures arrived, I had the task of endlessly arranging them for the Heritage tapestry. I spent hours lying back and gazing at various groupings for the fourteen-panel screen.

(Left) These inventive trees were among the dozens of categories which went into the Heritage screen.

Robert Buys then expertly mounted and hinged them. We were sponsored by the British Wool Marketing Board who sent the finished tapestry on a touring exhibition all over Britain and as far as Japan! The entire screen can now be seen at Chatsworth House in Derbyshire.

MY APPROACH TO NEEDLEPOINT

You might have guessed by now that this book is not for the technically minded looking for fancy stitches. Needlepoint for me is a vehicle for bringing personal colour into any interior. Like any craft, there are many ways to approach needlepoint designs and more rules than even fastidious embroidery guilds and learned books can teach you. I came to the subject without any preconceived ideas and certainly no rules. My first attempts had stitches going the

wrong way and knots and split threads. I still have a rough 'get-it-done-the-quickest-way' approach after twenty years' practice.

As in my knitting, I only use two basic stitches (tent stitch and long stitch) to carry as much colour as I want. Tent stitch is perfect for detailed work. With it you can think like a pointillist painter, making subtle transitions with sprays of coloured dots. When looking for the exuberance of rapid growth in a design, I use long stitch to fill in areas quickly. It is also ideal for mixing tones by running three-to-five colours together in a needle. This really is painting with a broad brush. With these simple techniques under your belt you can

concentrate on subject matter and the glorious world of colour. (See pages 152–157 for basic techniques.)

DESIGNING

Every good bit of decoration is like a piece of music. It has an emotional impact on some surface. Decoration worth its salt should make any object, from a wall to a snuff box, dance with inner movement. If a design from the past catches your eye and goes on delighting you after many viewings, it has life in it – not so common a trait in this world of ours. There are miles and miles of

stiff, deadly boring objects decorated to the hilt which are not at all lively. As I get longer in the tooth and time gets shorter, the urgency to produce the most entertaining, delicious and above all *lively* work is paramount. This statement of animation can be achieved simply by the arrangement of colours that sing in our environments. A pile of cushions, flowers in a jolly jug, a colourful cloth over a table, a carpet that

(Right) The harvest bowl long-stitch sketch which led on to the Harvest Bowl tapestry kit.

(Far right above) Many varieties of lichens can make wonderful subjects for needlepoint (see pages 140–141 for my lichen frame).

(Far right) This tent-stitch rendering of lichens was commissioned by a New York art dealer for a corner chair.

relates well with a couch can all make our lives harmonious and definitely far happier.

DESIGN SOURCES

In this media-bombarded twentieth century, sources for exciting design to help us

get started are thick on the ground. TV cameras enter beautifully decorated houses, palaces and museums all over the world, revealing elegant treasures to inspire us. Books and magazines abound in sources of colour and pattern to build a stimulating collection for the would-be designer. Exhibitions of painting and decorative arts and natural history in museums with posters and postcards help to develop our decorative eye for colour and pattern. Of course, many a good idea can come from the commonest occurrences – walls of stones or bricks, fruit laid out at the greengrocer, groups of people in the streets.

This book contains some of my favourite sources, from the Orient to Victorian paper scraps. I have charted a number of designs, giving specific yarns, so that you can reproduce these exactly. Many of my needlepoints can be obtained from Ehrman as kits, to save you having to read the charts and

pick out the yarns (see pages 150 and 158). Ultimately though, I hope that my personal unlimited-colour projects will inspire you to have a go at designing similar flights of fancy for yourself.

YOUR OWN DESIGNS

Designing need not be at all daunting. There are basic steps to producing handsome, colourful designs from any of the plethora of sources that fill our lives – a piece of china, photographs or illustrations, lichen-covered stone, butterflies and shells, or a bouquet of flowers. First, repeating

your childhood fantasies comes into play. How easy it was for us to pretend a brick was a cake or a daisy chain was a jewelled necklace. To stimulate your imagination, try laying leaves on a cushion to suggest patterns that can be stitched; or try cutting the shape of a chair from a sheet of paper and passing that over photographs or paint-

(Far left) My early Oriental arrangement tent-stitch tapestry measuring 1.7m/5½ft by 2.3m/7½ft. Some of my favourite china pots led to this design and a similar fabric for Designers' Guild in London.

(Above left) I keep thousands of postcards and small graphic references to help with designing and making colour choices.

(Left) Shells, particularly faded, sun-washed ones, are a delectable source of form and colour.

9

ings until a group of colours catches your eye. Another way to play with elements of design is to cut out forms from wallpaper samples or magazines, such as leaves, fruits and flowers, and arrange them until they 'click'. When I am really unsure, I pin these cut-outs to the chair or object that I want to cover and live with them for a bit.

The important thing is to choose sources that have a complex colouring which encourages the use of many shades of colour. This is the real secret of exciting needlepoint as opposed to the pedestrian variety

we see so often.

To begin your design take a scrap of paper and sketch the object you want to create – a lampshade, carpet or cushion cover. Then roughly draw the design you

(Above right) I like the chunky lace texture with these shells in my larger-than-life painting.

(Right) Detail of shell bedcover which I did with the help of artist Craig Biondi.

(Far right) A bird drawing from my design sketchbook.

want to reproduce up to scale. In other words, if doing a flower from a china vase onto a spectacles case, do you want it to fill the space with just one flower? Or do you want a background with another pattern showing, and the flower quite small and

perhaps repeated or placed off-centre? Lots of doodles will inspire you, so try drawing any outrageous thing that occurs to you. Never be timid at this stage of design – you may stumble on a good idea.

TRANSLATING SOURCES INTO NEEDLEPOINT

The important thing about working from found sources is the placing of the motifs and getting the scale right. It is rare that you can simply use the design as you find it. Bear in mind that the edges of cushions or

chair pieces are obscured when mounted. So do not have your most gorgeous details disappearing into seams or under chair arms. I have often done this, as I work right to the edges of my paper most of the time. I suppose it is better than being too cautious and having miles of boring one-colour grounds. You will notice that I did rich detail right to the edges of the blue orchard chair cover. If you looked at the finished chair (pages 29–31), you will see how a lot of detail does get lost. I still maintain that a rich, varied texture of pattern and colour is preferable to solid ground. If a subtle effect is wanted the ground can be done in very close-toned colours.

After choosing the best of my initial sketches, I usually do a rough drawing, the size I want the finished needlepoint to be. I sometimes paint this in watercolour to get an idea of the colour layout. Then I draw a bold outline around the main shapes in the design and lay this under the canvas for tracing. Using a waterproof pen, I trace the outlines of the design shapes onto the canvas, leaving a 5cm/2″ border of unused canvas around the edge. If you feel you might want to adjust a design as you go, then do the tracing in a paler colour, like orange or red, to start. The corrections can be drawn in a deeper colour, like dark brown or navy or green waterproof ink. Black is not a good idea, as it is difficult to see when stitching.

Be sure to keep a paper template of your original design. I use my sketch for this. It is important to save a template to help you stretch your needlepoint back to shape after stitching (see page 155). I do not use a

frame, so the work gets very distorted and needs stretching after it is completed. Working on a frame slows work down a bit, but it does keep the canvas in shape.

WORKING YOUR NEEDLEPOINT

Before stitching, the most important thing is to gather enough colours together to make a good start on your subject. I take the subject matter to the shop and match the yarns on the spot. If I am in doubt, I will press a strand of yarn onto the printed colour in my source material to see if it

melts into it. The mistake most people make when beginning to design from a source is to pick colours that are too dark. Each stitch creates a little shadow, so a slightly lighter colour often appears just the right shade when stitched. I always buy several shades of each colour, anyway, to make variations and shadings.

It is very important to have quite a few of your colours in crewel weight. This is about one-third the weight of regular tapestry yarn and is used for petit-point and embroidery. Crewel is invaluable when doing

subtle shadings, combining two or three colours in each stitch. It is also a life saver when you run out of a colour in full flow, miles from a shop. Just take two similar colours in crewel and you can make an amazing match that also brings a bit more richness to your work.

As you start to work on the colour stitches, you must cultivate the patience to stitch quite large areas of colours together before you can see if they are working properly. More often than not, the initial stages of a work can look like nothing on earth. Pinning the canvas up and standing back to study it is most important, when improvising colours. When stuck on a piece, I often pin it up on the wall across from the foot of my bed and lay back to read, work or sleep. Glancing up (or waking up in the morning), I often glimpse what needs to happen next. The work should talk to you if you let it. I often find myself taking quite a different direction than I originally intended. That is when the thrill of creating can get deliciously obsessive!

(Far left) I fall in love with the various flat shapes for upholstered chairs. Much of the detail at the edges gets lost when mounted, but I still fill the shape with colour.

(Left) The autumn landscape tapestry in progress (see page 85 for the finished tapestry). I am wearing one of my jumpers inspired by an old American patchwork quilt made of stamp-sized squares.

FRUITS AND VEGETABLES

IF fruits and vegetables did not have the mundane role of feeding us, they might be every bit as revered as flowers and trees. Painters through the ages have done their best to celebrate these handsome objects, and decorative art, from china to stencilled furnishings, abounds in good 'fruit-and-veg' sources.

Needlepoint is the perfect medium in which to capture the colour-highlights and shadows of fruits and vegetables. It can achieve an Old Master effect, such as that found in early Dutch still lifes, or a flat, stylized paper cut-out look, and many degrees in between.

You will see in this chapter that I grab as models for my needlepoints anything from a piece of wrapping paper to a china plate. One of my favourite sources of fruits is to be found in an elegantly decorated room in the harem in the Topkapi Palace in Istanbul. A painted frieze there consists of baskets and china bowls piled high with pears, apples, plums and figs. These pyramids of fruit surrounded by gold and red geometric borders are still striking and provide wonderful subjects for needlepoint.

■ (Right) The plum cushion in front of the elegantly toned Japanese screen.

■ (Far right) Fruit cushions in progress on garden steps set into Steve's collage of fruit cuttings.

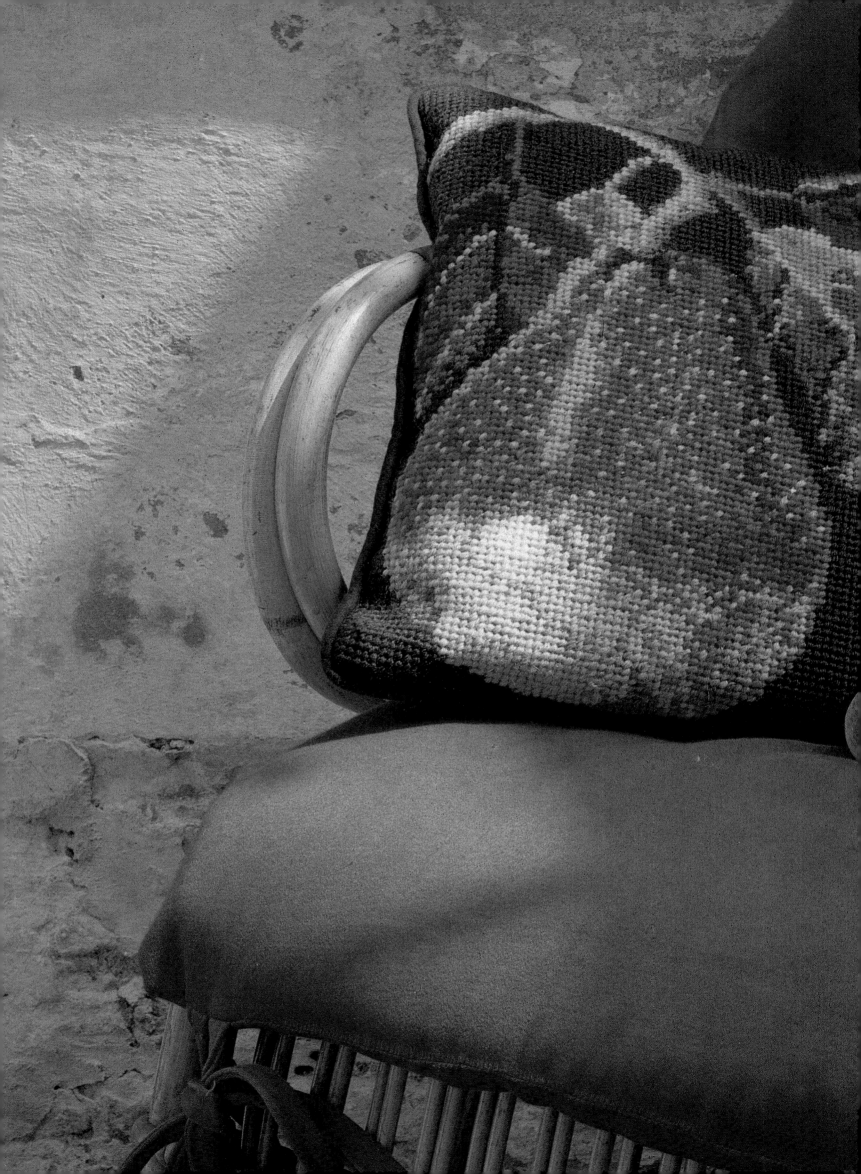

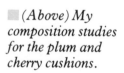 *(Above) My composition studies for the plum and cherry cushions.*

 *(Above right) Textile designer Susan Collier's kitchen, with her fabrics and collections of china, makes a lively setting for the apple and pear cushions.*

(Previous page) The little crab apples make the apple and pear needlepoints assume gigantic proportions.

FRUIT CUSHIONS

My apple, pear and cherry cushions were inspired by an excellent source book, *The Oxford Book of Food Plants*, full of watercolours of fruits and vegetables in rich detail and well-defined colours. Any fruit subjects would make handsome cushions, but the complex colourings of autumn fruit and turning leaves make them particularly luscious on a large scale – each piece becomes a landscape of dots, veins and blushes of colour. The plums were taken from a wrapping paper covered in Victorian paintings of fruit. I used it first as a source for a mural and later for the blue orchard chair (page 29).

MATERIALS FOR PEAR CUSHION

Appleton tapestry wool in the following colours and approximate amounts (see page 152):

- 226 (11m/12yd)
- 756 (18m/20yd)
- 703 (2.7m/3yd)
- 864 (18m/20yd)

- 251 (20m/22yd)
- 544 (20m/22yd)
- 243 (11m/12yd)
- 765 (14m/15yd)
- 843 (23m/25yd)
- 479 (6.5m/7yd)
- 708 (12m/13yd)
- 932 (20m/22yd)
- 934 (12m/13yd)
- 142 (11m/12yd)
- 204 (16m/18yd)
- 205 (35m/38yd)
- 647 (137m/150yd)

7-mesh double-thread or interlocked canvas 47cm/18¾" square
70cm/¾yd of 90cm/36" backing fabric and matching thread
1.5m/1¾yd of piping cord
30cm/12" zip fastener (optional)
Finished needlepoint measures approximately 37cm/14¾" square.

MATERIALS FOR PLUM CUSHION

Appleton tapestry wool in the following colours and approximate amounts (see page 152):

- 101 (24m/26yd)
- 104 (18m/20yd)
- 832 (20m/22yd)
- 402 (27m/30yd)

- ◼ 105 (11m/12yd)
- ◼ 106 (41m/45yd)
- ◼ 453 (6.5m/7yd)
- ◼ 745 (15m/16yd)
- ◼ 462 (3.7m/4yd)
- ◼ 227 (8m/9yd)
- ◼ 956 (9m/10yd)
- ◼ 475 (8m/9yd)

- ◼ 547 (16m/18yd)
- ◼ 548 (8m/9yd)
- ◼ 242 (6.5m/7yd)
- ◼ 251 (20m/22yd)
- ◼ 421 (8m/9yd)
- ◼ 767 (18m/20yd)
- ◼ 765 (8m/9yd)
- ☐ 647 (137m/150yd)

7-mesh double-thread or interlocked canvas
48cm/19¼″ square
70cm/¾yd of 90cm/36″ backing fabric and
matching thread
1.5m/1¾yd of piping cord
30cm/12″ zip fastener (optional)
*Finished needlepoint measures approximately
38cm/15¼″ square.*

(Opposite page)
The boldness of the
plums works well in a
modern setting with a
fresh, bright palette.

WORKING PEAR AND PLUM CUSHIONS

The pear chart (page 17) is 104 stitches wide by 104 stitches high. The plum chart (page 18) is 107 stitches wide by 107 stitches high. For each, mark the outline onto the canvas and make a template (see page 155). Following the chart (see page 154), work the embroidery in tent stitch using *two strands* of tapestry wool together. Lastly, work the background for each of the cushions in 647. Block the finished needlepoint (see page 155). Cut and sew the backing and piping (see page 156).

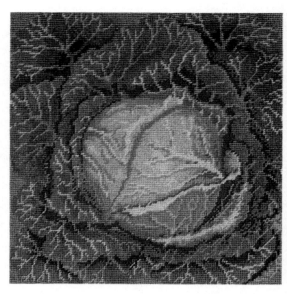

CABBAGES AND CAULIFLOWERS

I was once asked to paint a mural in a
farmhouse in Scotland. It was for the sitting
room, and I amazed my hostess by suggest-
ing I depict one of the gorgeous cabbages
her husband was growing in their field.
I painted it three times larger than life
over the fireplace, and surrounded it with
old, green-leaf plates. The effect was quite
elegant and heartily appreciated.

On another mural commission, however,
the results were not so well received. I
painted a purple cabbage into a decorative
flower-and-fruit border for a landscape. The
commissioner then painted over my three-
month effort the day after I finished it!

Purple or red cabbages are fabulous objects, with deep, mysterious colours. I once
heard of a garden planted with rows of
purple cabbages and lined with chunks of
black coal – how elegant it must have been!
A lunch party I went to in an English
country house had a glorious decoration of
several purple and green cabbages on an old
French tapestry. No flowers were needed.

When looking for a round, leafy form to
go with the cabbage mat, my eye alighted on
a cauliflower in a gardening book. The
radiating leaves and the big, glowing,
creamy whiteness of the vegetable made a
good contrast to the cabbage. The graphic
strength of the leaf veins were a good
starting point and, once I had stitched
these, I filled in the deepest of the shadows
and worked out through the softer greens.

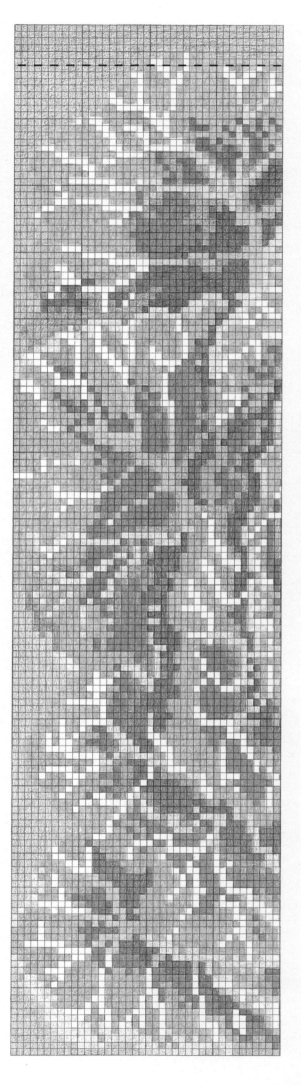

It always amazes me how easy it is to create the illusion of shadowy layers with so few colours. I kept the centre of the cauliflower very light for a fresh, white glow.

MATERIALS FOR CABBAGE CUSHION

Appleton tapestry wool in the following colours and approximate amounts (see page 152):

	831 (84m/91yd)		544 (26m/28yd)
	832 (37m/40yd)		641 (22m/24yd)
	834 (39m/43yd)		643 (23m/25yd)
	421 (27m/29yd)		873 (22m/24yd)
	423 (8m/9yd)		881 (14m/15yd)
	425 (3m/4yd)		601 (22m/24yd)

10-mesh double-thread or interlocked canvas 49cm/19½" square
50cm/½yd of 90cm/36" felt backing fabric
30cm/12" zip fastener (optional)
Finished needlepoint measures approximately 38cm/15¼" by 39cm/15½".

MATERIALS FOR CAULIFLOWER CUSHION

Appleton tapestry wool in the following colours and approximate amounts (see page 152):

	831 (81m/88yd)		641 (16m/18yd)
	832 (30m/32yd)		643 (32m/35yd)
	834 (35m/38yd)		544 (14m/15yd)
	523 (34m/37yd)		421 (11m/12yd)
	877 (12m/13yd)		423 (14m/15yd)
	874 (17m/19yd)		601 (16m/18yd)
	873 (35m/38yd)		

■ *(Right) You could join two cauliflower squares to make an eye-catching shopping bag.*

■ *(Far right) Dining on a cauliflower would be a fresh experience.*

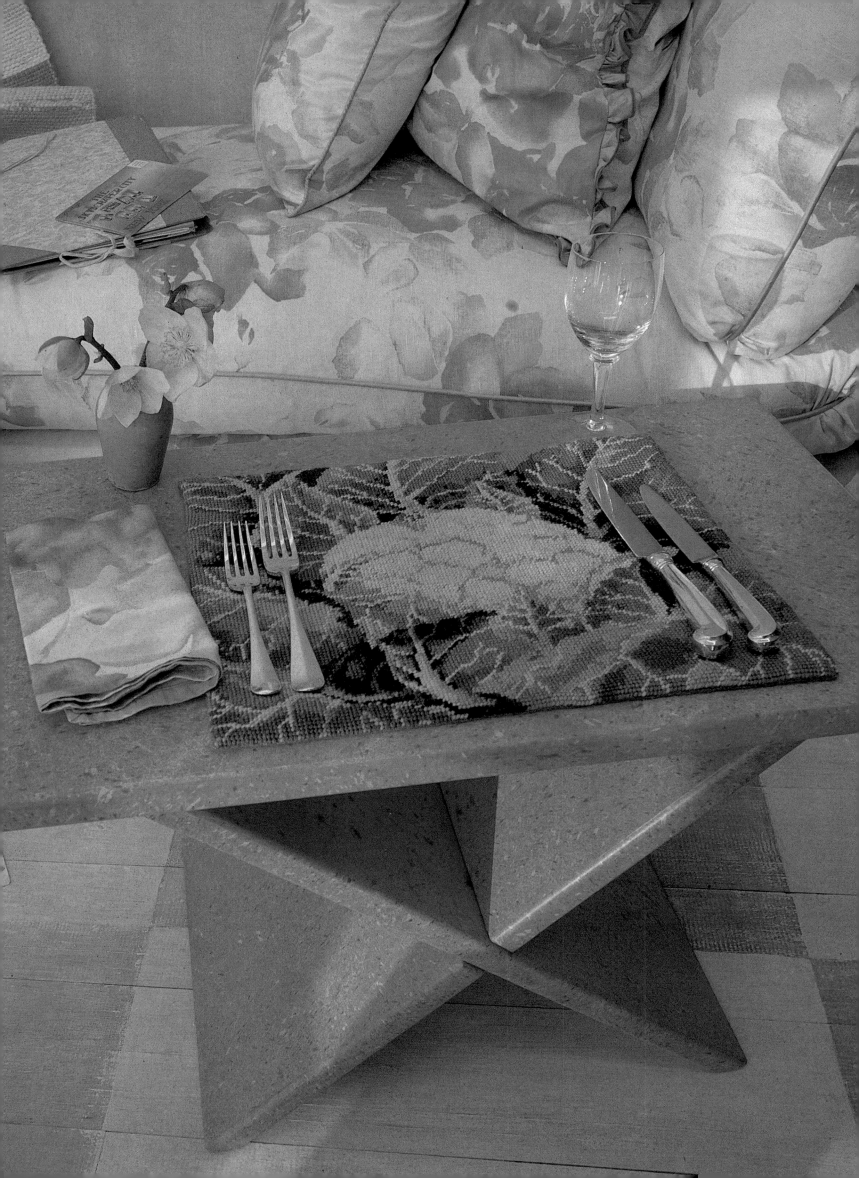

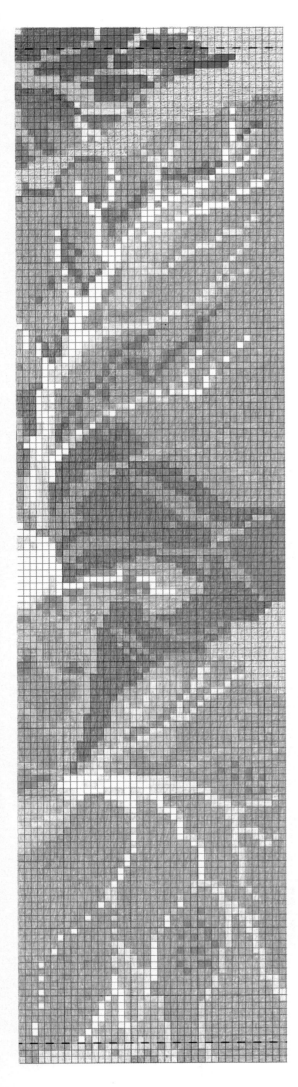

10-mesh double-thread or interlocked
canvas 49cm/19½" square
50cm/½yd of 90cm/36" felt backing fabric
30cm/12" zip fastener (optional)
*Finished needlepoint measures approximately
38cm/15¼" by 39cm/15½".*

WORKING CABBAGE AND CAULIFLOWER CUSHIONS

The cabbage cushion chart (page 23) is 153
stitches wide by 155 stitches high. The
cauliflower cushion chart (page 26) is 153
stitches wide by 155 stitches high. For each,
mark the outline onto the canvas and make
a template (see page 155). Following the
chart (see page 154), work the embroidery
in tent stitch using *one strand* of tapestry
wool. Block the finished needlepoint (see
page 155). Cut and sew the backing (see
page 156).

WORKING CABBAGE AND CAULIFLOWER PLACEMATS

The placemats are 153 stitches wide by 149
stitches high. Omit the six top rows of the
cabbage chart and the three top and three
bottom rows of the cauliflower chart (see
dotted lines). For each, mark the outline
onto the canvas and make a template. Work
the embroidery and finish as for the cushions, omitting the zip fastener.

*(Below) These
cushion designs would
make an amusing
carpet, perhaps
combined with
cabbage roses from the
flower trellis carpet on
page 56.*

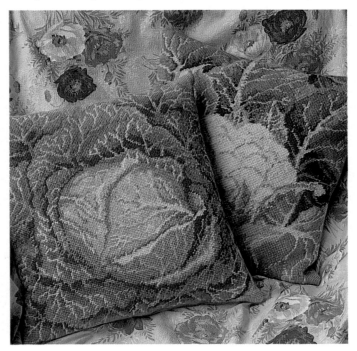

27

BLUE ORCHARD CHAIR

When I was commissioned to do this chair there was little in the way of a colour scheme to work with. The owner was thinking of re-doing the curtains, but had not settled on the exact colour and pattern. She had a painting with rich blues and reds that she was fond of, so we started from that.

My first step was to gather together pictures of deep-toned fruits, from books, magazines and even wrapping paper. I knew dark plums, cherries, grapes and maroon apples would work a treat on an inky royal blue ground. Emerald and forest greens in the leaves, with bright red and crisp paler green highlights, would complete the colour story. My intention was to avoid bright yellows or ochres to keep the blues and reds clean and 'singing'.

I did not draw out the whole composition in detail on paper, but just made a sketch to organize my ideas and to show the client. This sketching is like thinking aloud. When you put your different sources together, you can reject the elements that distract from your artistic vision. For instance, you will see from the finished chair that the scale is much finer in the original sketch. This is because I did the stitching with double tapestry yarn on a 7-mesh canvas. To get

■ *(Right) My original watercolour sketch for the blue orchard chair.*

■ *(Far right) My inspiration for the blue orchard chair came from many sources – the apple and leaf from a picture in a book, the plums from a wrapping paper, the grapes from a painting and the leaves from a china plate.*

■ *(Right) For the back of the chair I designed a classic plaid needlepoint, using the predominant colours of the fruit panels.*

■ *(Below) The fruit appears jewel-like on the royal blue ground.*

the detail definition I wanted, each leaf and fruit needed to be larger in scale. Before beginning the needlepoint, I collected all my source material around me and drew the outlines of the different bits onto the canvas so that they overlapped or sat next to each other, looking as if they all belonged in the same composition.

When the outlines of the fruits and leaves were complete, I stitched in a bit of background by starting with the deepest blues around each form. Then I built up an area of luminous lighter blues, shading it out with about five shades of blue and a little dark lavender, run here and there to warm up the blue. Once the ground was estab-

lished in a corner of the chair, I started to fill in some fruit and leaves in that area, to see if the background worked. I stitched the veins on the leaves first, then the shadows to create the layered feeling, and finished with the highest colours in the leaves. For the most part, I kept the colours higher and brighter than I usually do. Although working very close to my source material, I altered the colours slightly to make them all gel together. What pleases me most about the finished chair is how the deep, glowing tones of the wood come alive with the jewel colours of the needlepoint!

(Above) The burgundy binding around the completed needlepoint is a well-balanced finish.

31

FISH AND FOWL

THE worlds of birds and the sea are so filled with good design material that one hardly knows where to begin. Certainly, I am only giving you a taste of the thousands of forms, colours and patterns that abound amongst their themes. I have concentrated on shells and eggs because their colouring is so appropriate to the soft, gentle tones of certain interiors. These objects are classically beautiful, and I have often painted them in my still lifes.

For years I have harboured the dream of decorating a complete room with nothing but domestic animals in tapestries. Ducks, with their handsome shapes and coloured feather patterns, have always featured strongly in my image of this project. From poring over bird books and watching the beautifully filmed wildlife documentaries on television, I have been alerted to the wealth of ideas in birdlife.

Fish are not well served here when you consider how startlingly beautiful and

■ *(Below) The faded shells create an Italian fresco colouring in the scallop shell lampshade.*

■ *(Right) Robert Buy's sensitive, rubbed painting on the wooden base echoes the fresco colouring perfectly.*

varied their markings and shapes can be. I leave that field wide open to you. Any book on fish should give you wonderful subject matter. Look to the Orient again for superb paintings and china decoration, or to embroidery for simplified fish.

Designing fish and fowl needlepoints from actual models – shells, eggs, fish in aquariums, birds in the farmyard or garden – can be wonderfully inspiring, but also quite daunting for someone not used to painting and drawing from life. It is always easier to start working from a recorded image – a photograph, painting, lithograph or, easiest of all, an embroidered or woven textile. These two-dimensional representations supply a constant light source on the object and, in the case of illustrations or embroidery, the colours will be somewhat simplified.

SCALLOP SHELL LAMPSHADE

I started this design intending to be very realistic in getting all the little markings and shadows as accurate as possible, but I soon saw that the scale chosen would not allow for such clear details. So I began simplifying the shells, emphasizing the fan shape by using one colour for the rays contrasted with a lighter colour in between. Then I added a touch of shadow colour where possible, varying the shells' colours from greys and pinks to goldy browns and maintaining clarity from one shell to another. I stayed away from any really clean bright

colours, keeping to the dusty tones of Italian frescoes. The difficulty was to stay light in tone, and only go as dark as a mid-grey or brown to keep the faded, sun-washed look. Dark tones would have cut the design with too much contrast. I wanted to create a lamp that would harmonize with the objects I collect and hardly be noticed.

When sorting out my colours, I first determine which the darkest and lightest shades are. The lightest is usually not clean white, but a cream or beigey colour; the darkest not black, but some much softer shade. Studying your source material, you can learn to pick out the darkest dark and lightest light tones, and to design within these limits. Most distortions in colour schemes are caused by arbitrary contrast.

MARBLE CONE SHELL

Unlike the scallop shell needlepoint, a high contrast was the very effect I was after for the marble cone shell. Black and white is one of those eternal themes that injects a sharp accent into design arrangements. From primitive African beadwork (page 38) to slick modern statements, this theme reappears throughout history. These little shells on their grey ground should fit in with modern or antique settings. I have often painted this shell into still lifes and never tire of its confident freshness.

I drew out and stitched one shell at the centre, then gave outlined shells to my assistant to stitch. She filled them in with all

(Right) I started the marble cone shells on a 10-mesh canvas but the texture was too crude, so I went for a finer canvas.

(Opposite page) Strong contrast in shells can be very effective for small objects like this shade. The striped shell at the base of the lamp would make an excellent needlepoint.

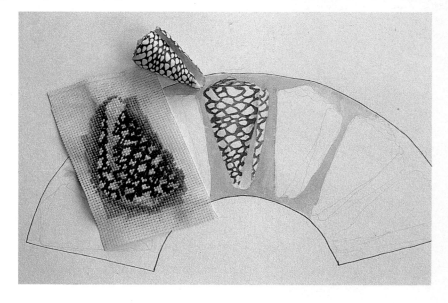

the variations you see – with the little shadow at the edges and the blush of peach interiors. Each shape holds its own. You will notice that my first attempt at stitching was on 10-mesh canvas. This produced too crude a texture to capture the delicacy of these little shells to my satisfaction, unless done on a much larger scale. So I turned to petit-point canvas and crewel yarns. The fine canvas takes a lot longer to work but creates a sharp, highly focused texture. Try the shell chart on 10-mesh or 7-mesh canvas, as a bold cushion or border for a carpet.

I seldom work on petit-point canvas because it is very time-consuming, but I often think of designs for this delicate texture. A little doll's face on this scale would be beautiful. I once did a very detailed petit-point doll's chair 26cm/10″ high. The back was a group of trees with the seat showing stones in a meadow divided by a winding brook.

MATERIALS FOR MARBLE CONE SHELL MOTIF

Appleton crewel wool in the following colours and approximate amounts for each motif (see page 152):

861 (0.3m/¼yd)		588 (0.9m/1yd)	
205 (0.3m/¼yd)		584 (3.7m/4yd)	
182 (0.5m/½yd)		965 (0.9m/1yd)	
992 (4.6m/5yd)		963 (6.4m/7yd)	
202 (0.5m/½yd)		961 (0.9m/1yd)	
702 (0.9m/1yd)			

18-mesh mono canvas in desired size
Finished charted motif measures approximately 7.5cm/3″ by 12.5cm/5″.

WORKING MARBLE CONE SHELL MOTIF

The shell chart is 54 stitches wide by 88 stitches high. The petit-point embroidery is worked in tent stitch using *one strand* of crewel wool. The motif can be repeated on a larger gauge canvas to make a cushion cover, or used as a repeated motif border for another petit-point design. The more adventurous embroiderer may like to make a petit-point lampshade, for which a lampshade frame is required.

First make a paper template of your lampshade frame and trace the shape onto the canvas so that the centre section is on the straight grain of the canvas. Work the first motif at the centre of the lampshade, following the chart. For the other shell motifs trace the shell shape onto paper, then outline the shapes on the canvas (see page 155). Fill in the other motifs, using the first motif as a guide for colours, and letting variations occur. Block the finished needlepoint (see page 155). Trim the canvas and sew to the frame. Then line the shade with paper and trim top and bottom with cord.

(Right) You will see from the stretched-out shade that each shell comes out delightfully different. This was achieved simply by drawing the shape and pattern of each shell with a waterproof pen onto the canvas and stitching with variations.

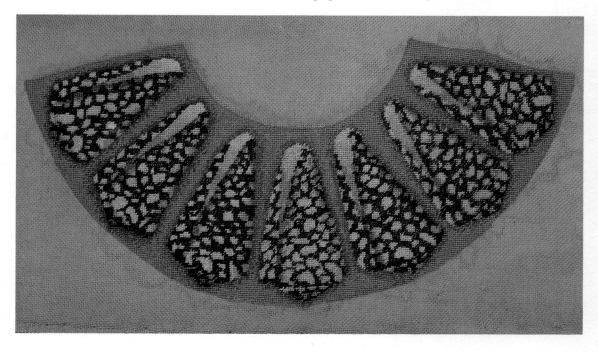

(Overleaf) My lobster bag with beaded gourds from the Cameroons. The pinky silver-fish would make a handsome subject for needlepoint.

(Above) I enjoy the way the piano keys and the straw box echo the black-and-white chequerboard of the needlepoint.

LOBSTER BAG

I took this lovely boiled lobster and crab from a photograph of ingredients in a cookbook. I was looking for a big, complex shape, and this handsome red creature was just the ticket. Drawing the shapes on paper and cutting them out helped me to place them on the bag. I then drew an outline of each creature on the canvas and worked from the photographs. The black-and-white chequerboard background was suggested by Steve, who was thinking of fishmongers' tile counters. For a softer contrast, I used a combination of brown and dark-grey crewel

40

threads and off-white, instead of hard black and white.

The crab was the more interesting to stitch. There are about nineteen colours in its shell alone – maroons, sage-greens, ochres, pinks, merge with grey-browns. This kind of richness of colour can only be achieved with a great many actual tones and combinations of crewel threads. Most kits cannot afford to include so many colours (there are at least thirty in this bag). This is the beauty of designing for yourself – the indulgence of unlimited colour. Remember always to use many tones of each colour, wherever possible.

SHELL HEADBOARD

A Californian furniture designer, Morris Sheppard, asked me to do a special needlepoint headboard for a new bed commission he had received. It was for a house on a beautiful stretch of California coastline, and the brief was only to keep my colours light and creamy.

I had a large collection of old, faded shells with washed-out, creamy colourings and felt they would be a good theme. Picking shells which had distinct shapes, or bold colourings, which would read easily, helped me to avoid too much realistic shading. I arranged them on a breadboard and worked directly from them as a still life, after outlining the shapes several times larger that life onto the canvas. The breadboard, with its carefully arranged shells, was easily stored under my work table, out of harm's way when not needed.

Using long stitch on 7-mesh canvas, I could use five or six different coloured crewel threads together to create a silky look. The fragile, pastel clouds echoed the shell colours to make one harmonious texture. The references for the clouds came from various classical paintings. Your imagination really comes into play when making composites of elements from several sources. Imagine how different the background would have been with a red-and-pink sunset, or a mountain and seascape in slate-greys. By juggling with sources in this way, you can make any piece of needlepoint furniture really harmonize with the existing elements of your room. Colours from the rug or the lampshade, or even from the garden outside, can be echoed in the needlepoint.

(Left) This shell headboard was stitched in random long stitch on 7-mesh canvas. The whole piece measures 76cm/ 30" by 5.5m/6ft.

ROOSTER TEA COSY

I have always been startled by the beauty of domestic animals. As a child visiting farms in California, I remember well how the colours and elegant curves of roosters' feathers would rivet my attention. For this small tea cosy, I picked the bold black-and-white colouring of a silver-laced wyandotte cock. My reference is a plate from the *Illustrated Book of Poultry* with its Victorian paintings of fancy roosters and hens. It is a superb source for needlepoint projects. The clear details and colours in the illustrations are easy to translate for your own uses.

This tea-cosy design could be used for a cushion with a rounded top. Alternatively, you could simply extend the fence to make the top square, or add contrasting colour

■ *(Left) The bold tumbling-box pattern makes a superb ground for the rooster tea cosy.*

■ *(Below) This illustration was the source for my black-and-white rooster tea cosy.*

(Above) Domestic birds, especially with bold markings, come out well in needlepoint. I collect ideas from life or illustrations, by sketching them in my notebooks.

corners. Done with double yarn on a 7-mesh canvas, it would make a handsome chairback, or seat, or centre of a carpet! Inspired by Chinese drawings, the wicker fence is very simplified but creates quite a realistic effect.

MATERIALS FOR ROOSTER TEA COSY

Appleton tapestry wool in the following colours and approximate amounts (see page 152):

☐	992 (68m/74yd)	▨	923 (8m/9yd)
▦	184 (87m/95yd)	▫	461 (41m/45yd)
■	976 (68m/74yd)	▨	945 (5.5m/6yd)
▨	763 (87m/95yd)	▨	503 (5.5m/6yd)
▫	693 (56m/61yd)	▨	428 (8m/9yd)
▨	853 (5.5m/6yd)	■	993 (68m/74yd)

25g/1oz of extra tapestry wool in 503 *or* a matching scarlet yarn for pompom
10-mesh double-thread or interlocked canvas 84cm/34″ by 44cm/17½″
40cm/½yd of 90cm/36″ lining fabric and matching thread
1m/40″ of cord for edging
Piece of cardboard for pompom templates
Finished needlepoint measures approximately 32cm/13″ by 34cm/13½″ across each side.

WORKING ROOSTER TEA COSY

The tea cosy is worked in two identical pieces. The chart is 129 stitches wide by 135 stitches high. Mark the outline onto the canvas for the first side and make a template (see page 155). Following the chart (see page 154), work the embroidery in tent stitch using *one strand* of tapestry wool. Repeat for second side. Block the finished needlepoints (see page 155). Cut two pieces of lining the same size as the needlepoint plus a 1.5cm/⅝″ seam allowance. With the right sides facing, sew the lining together leaving the lower edge open. Sew the needlepoints together in the same way. Trim canvas and turn right side out. Sew on cord along needlepoint seam, leaving 1.5cm/⅝″ extra at ends to turn into hem. Insert lining, turn under lower edges of lining and needlepoint and cord, and stitch with invisible seam. (The tea cosy can be lined with polyester padding if desired for added insulation.)

For the pompom, first make four circular cardboard templates 9cm/3½″ in diameter. Cut a circle 2.5cm/1″ in diameter in the centre of two of the templates. Place the two templates with the holes on top of each other and wrap the scarlet yarn for the pompom round and round the templates through the centre hole. The more yarn used, the firmer the pompom will be. Break off the yarn. Cut a 30 cm/12″ length of yarn and set aside. Press the yarn-wrapped templates between the two circular templates. Holding the templates tightly at the centre, cut the yarn on the templates around the outer edge of the templates, so that the tips of the scissors slide between the two inner templates while cutting. Wrap the length of yarn around the centre hole between the templates, so that all of the strands are

(Right) The sketch for my pheasant cushion.

(Far right) The finished pheasant cushion.

(Below right) My rooster cushion.

(Below far right) The fish in the lily pond is a design idea that I have not yet used. It could make an interesting cushion.

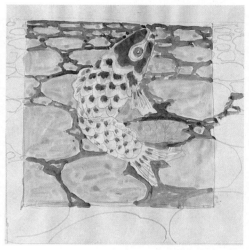

caught around the centre. Wrap the yarn around the centre a second time, and pull tightly. Secure with a knot, leaving long, loose ends. Remove the templates. Trim the pompom and stitch to top of the tea cosy, using the long, loose ends.

PHEASANT AND ROOSTER CUSHIONS

Early American decoration in the form of painted furniture, chintzes and crewel embroidery led to the pheasant design. It was first commissioned by Rosemary Miln for *Good Housekeeping* magazine. The boldness and simple childlike quality make it easy to draw and fun to stitch. Its layout is quite a good one for any number of different subjects. A turkey or duck with such a bold border in different colours would be very handsome.

The rooster cushion is yet another inspi-

ration from the *Illustrated Book of Poultry*. If you fancy a more textured background, the wicker fence from page 42 could be added.

The pheasant cushion can be obtained in kit form from Ehrman (see pages 150 and 158).

ORIENTAL FISH CUSHION

Japanese decoration has always attracted my designer's eye. The Japanese reverence for natural subjects, flowers, animals and fish is plain to see in millions of stylish examples. They have the knack of elegantly simplifying their subjects in a way that is a gift to a needlepoint designer.

This joyful fish was inspired by an 18th-century ceramic perfume container. The flowers and waves were borrowed from Japanese Kabuki costumes. This cushion is available as a kit (see page 158), so is necessarily limited in the number of colours. At least ten more could be used to advantage to give more tones of colour to flowers, sea and fish scales. Try doing your own version of the fish cushion in completely different colours.

DUCK CUSHIONS

Early English, French and Dutch tapestries and ceramics alerted me to the beauty of simple domestic birds such as roosters, hens, geese and ducks. Like fruits and vegetables, their very commonness in our lives sometimes makes us blasé about their elegant shapes and feather patterns. I have often drawn these animals in natural history museums, where I am most grateful for the stillness of my models!

■ *(Left) This is my original artwork for the oriental fish cushion kit.*

■ *(Below) The stitched canvas.*

(Right) These are both studies from natural history museums.

The world of ducks is so full of variety and contrasting styles that one could easily work from them alone for years without exhausting the freshness of the subject. Since Steve suggested I do these shaped duck cushions, I have noticed duck decoys in ceramic or wood everywhere in people's

houses. Like other 10-mesh designs in this book, these could be done larger by doubling the yarns and using 7-mesh canvas. It would be very effective to have a larger set scaled up to go with the smaller. If you prefer not to do your duck cushions as cutout shapes you could drop them into a background of ripples of water in grey-blues.

For that matter, there are wonderful ducks from China with exotic colour schemes that would make good designs for an unlimited yarn palette.

MATERIALS FOR GARGANEY DUCK
Appleton tapestry wool in the following colours and approximate amounts (see page 152):

473 (16m/18yd)		956 (16m/18yd)	
961 (6m/7yd)		584 (16m/18yd)	
964 (9m/10yd)		992 (28m/31yd)	
966 (5m/6yd)		461 (2.5m/3yd)	
861 (14m/15yd)		742 (9m/10yd)	

765 (18m/19yd)		744 (2.5m/3yd)	
184 (14m/15yd)		223 (4m/5yd)	
872 (4m/5yd)			

10-mesh double-thread or interlocked canvas 32cm/13″ by 51cm/20¼″
40cm/½yd of 90cm/36″ backing fabric and matching thread
25cm/10″ zip fastener (optional)
Finished needlepoint measures approximately 22cm/9″ by 41cm/16¼″ across widest points.

MATERIALS FOR PINTAIL DUCK
Appleton tapestry wool in the following colours and approximate amounts (see page 152):

982 (14m/15yd)		645 (2.5m/3yd)	
963 (14m/15yd)		183 (9m/10yd)	
964 (11m/12yd)		184 (6m/7yd)	
966 (5m/6yd)		186 (2.5m/3yd)	
121 (20m/21yd)		992 (28m/31yd)	
861 (9m/10yd)		583 (2.5m/3yd)	
875 (20m/21yd)		588 (11m/12yd)	
841 (18m/19yd)			

10-mesh double-thread or interlocked canvas 38cm/15″ by 52cm/20½″
40cm/½yd of 90cm/36″ backing fabric and matching thread
25cm/10″ zip fastener (optional)
Finished needlepoint measures approximately 28cm/11″ by 42cm/16½″ across widest points.

WORKING DUCK CUSHIONS

The garganey duck chart (page 50) is 163 stitches wide and 89 stitches high across its widest points. The pintail duck chart (page 51) is 166 stitches wide and 110 stitches high across its widest points. For each, mark the outline onto the canvas and make a template (see page 155). To read the chart turn the book sideways so that the duck's back is at the top of the chart (see page 154). Following the chart, work in tent stitch using *one strand* of tapestry wool. Block the finished needlepoint (see page 155). Cut and sew the backing (see page 156).

◼ *(Below) The restrained palette of greys and browns blends well with fabrics like the piece of antique African weaving.*

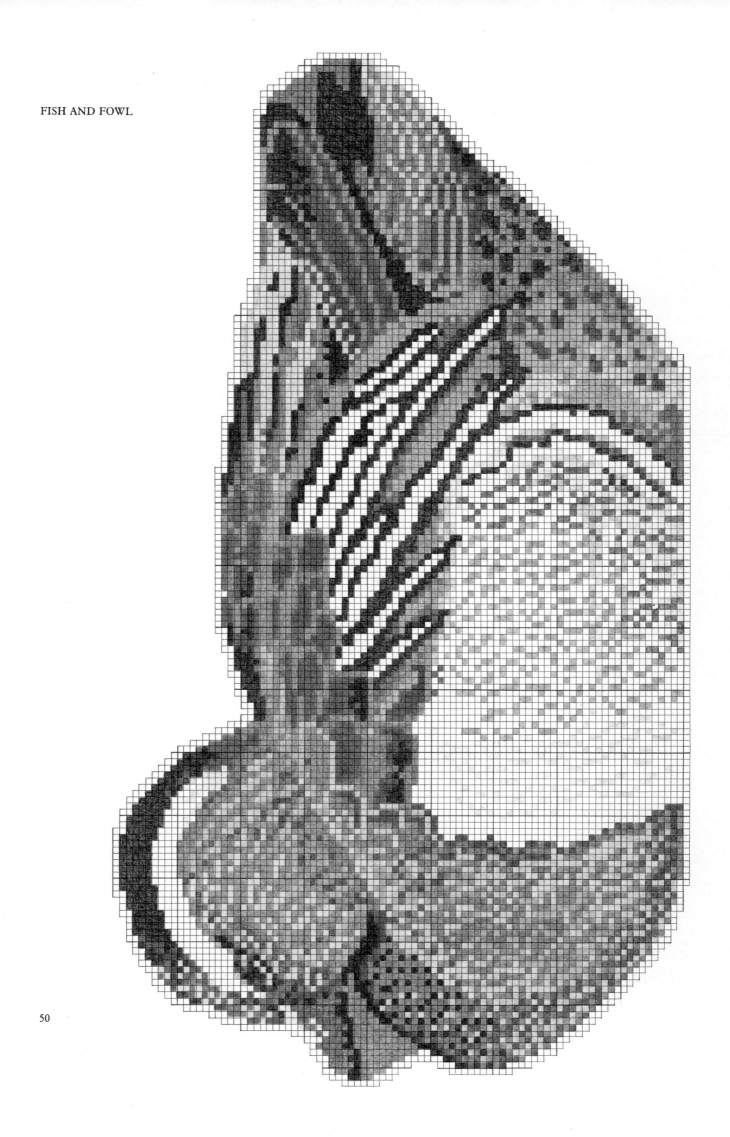

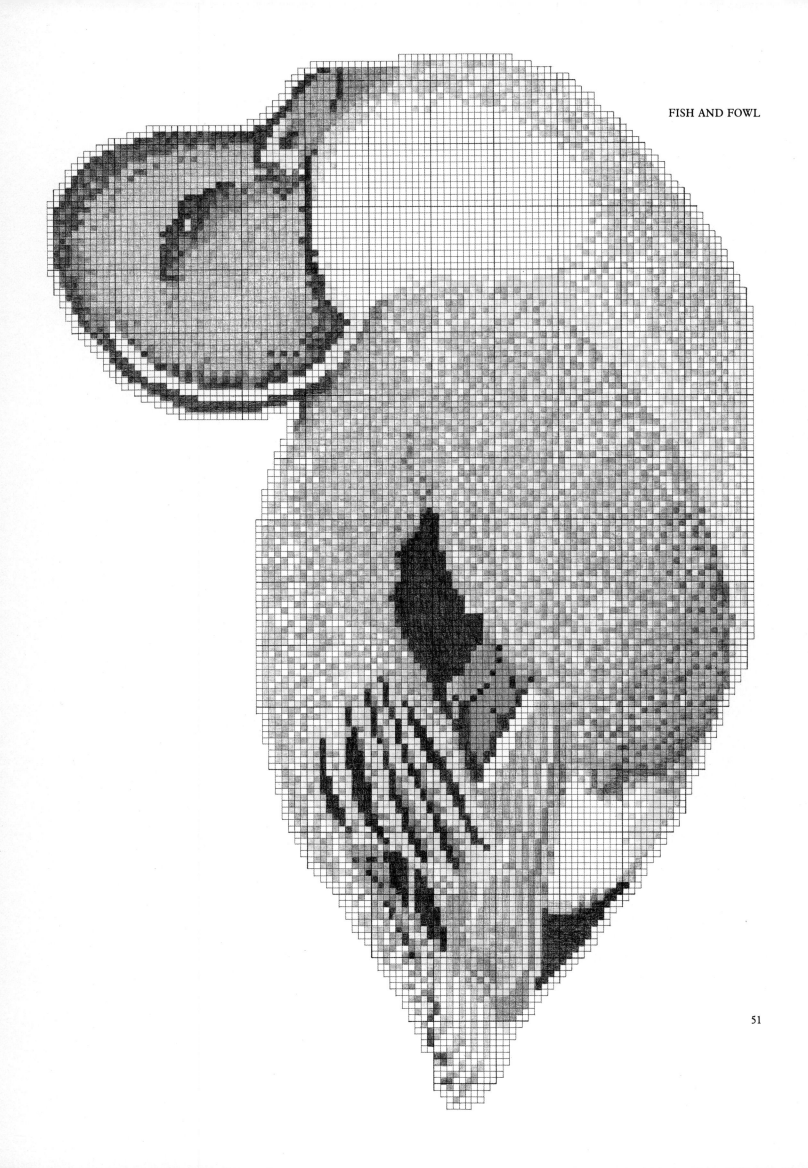

EGG POT HOLDER

I do not know what it is about eggs but they have always fascinated me. Years ago when I first came to England, I did a series of white-on-white still lifes using old china found in nearby Portobello Market. I often did paintings of eggs in white bowls or on off-white rumpled clothes. Later I discovered a wonderful set of postcards of birds' eggs in London's Natural History Museum which inspired this pot holder.

The variety of speckles, colours and sizes of these eggs always gives me a thrill. They are as beautiful as any gem stone to my eye. The merest suggestion of shadow here gives these quite a three-dimensional effect. The secret is to use as much colour variation as possible, while keeping tones very muted.

Cushions or tea cosies of baskets of eggs would be amusing and handsome. I would also like to see an egg lampshade, similar in layout to the one on page 35. Speckled eggs in a row on a grey ground would be quite elegant as well and not the sort of thing often seen! Any good book on birds' eggs should give you clear source material.

■ *(Below) Detail from one of my early still lifes.*

■ *(Right) The basket-of-eggs pot holder.*

FLOWERS AND FOLIAGE

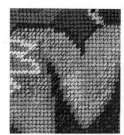 FOR sheer variety the world of flowers and leaves has few rivals for the decorative artist. From the subtlest washy tones and shapes to vibrant, full-blown forms, this theme has fed the imagination of artisans in every part of the world since humans first started to embellish their surroundings. Whether depicted in simple, childlike forms or in the most refined realism, flowers rarely fail to captivate the viewer. It would have been easy indeed to deal with nothing but flower themes in this book. There are few other symbols that so potently bring the flavour and nostalgia of the great ornamental traditions of Europe and the Orient to our lives.

The media bring us a constant flow of examples on porcelain, fabrics and painted furniture, so why not include what we fancy in our needlepoint? I often prefer to interpret a theme from a different medium in needlepoint – say from a porcelain jug design, or a mosaic table top – to see how it changes and often gains a new identity in wool or silk.

In this chapter I have tried for the main part to pick floral subjects that are fairly simple in structure to show how easy it is to design for yourself. Even the seemingly complex realistic flowers have a formula that is easy to learn. They usually begin with blushes of deep colour at bases of petals, becoming lighter towards edges. For an easy start in designing for needlepoint try taking flowers from china or old wallpapers where the colouring has been simplified for you. Oriental embroidery is filled with delectable uses of simple flower shapes. The fan throw (page 115) has three good examples of the rich variety of styles in Japanese floral decoration.

FLOWER TRELLIS CARPET
Here we have an unashamed romp in grand

■ (Right) Here are many of the sources I use constantly in my design work. The gold plate is a Portobello Market find. The seed-packet flowers figure in the flower trellis carpet, as do subjects from the old paintings, centre and top right. The large lily-like flower is printed on a Russian fabric and the cut-out flowers are from a horticultural diary.

 *(Above) The dark china, kelim and Victorian reproduction masks make a good setting for the carpet.*

opera! I selected overblown, strongly defined flowers from old paintings, flower studies, seed packets and a Victorian photo album for this striking carpet. Having to limit such a production to twenty-five colours (so I could offer it to you as a kit – see page 158) was the hardest task. If I had been

creating this needlepoint as a one-off commission, I would have used upwards of a hundred colours. It would have been impossible to fit the entire chart for the carpet into the book, but I was determined to include it somehow. So I chose a section of the carpet that I thought would make a beautiful large cushion. I moved one blooming cabbage rose into the ensemble and extended the trellis along a second edge. For a smaller cushion about 39cm/ 15½″ square, work on 10-mesh canvas with single yarn.

If you are attempting my floral trellis carpet or cushion and you are feeling adventurous, do add colours, particularly shades of beige and pale greys, in place of some areas of off-whites. This softening of the white areas would give a less contrasting effect in the larger light areas. If, on the other hand, you want an altogether less dramatic mood, simply replace the black with a silver-grey and change the trellis to shades of ochre-golds. The effect should be quite sunny!

MATERIALS FOR FLOWER TRELLIS CUSHION

Appleton tapestry wool in the following colours and approximate amounts (see page 152):

- 956 (32m/35yd)
- 184 (78m/85yd)
- 765 (32m/35yd)
- 464 (19m/21yd)
- 463 (7.3m/8yd)
- 992 (41m/45yd)
- 474 (15m/16yd)
- 476 (20m/22yd)
- 551 (26m/29yd)
- 553 (12m/13yd)

- 462 (16m/17yd)
- 641 (18m/20yd)
- 644 (18m/20yd)
- 647 (17m/19yd)
- 402 (27m/29yd)
- 941 (32m/35yd)
- 943 (27m/29yd)
- 944 (27m/29yd)
- 505 (40m/44yd)
- 504 (48m/53yd)
- 502 (55m/60yd)
- 105 (15m/16yd)
- 103 (15m/16yd)
- 102 (12m/13yd)
- 993 (124m/136yd)

7-mesh double-thread or interlocked canvas 65cm/26″ square
70cm/¾yd of 90cm/36″ black backing fabric and matching thread
2.2m/2½yd of cord for edging (optional)
45cm/18″ zip fastener (optional)
Finished needlepoint measures approximately 55cm/22″ square.

WORKING FLOWER TRELLIS CUSHION

The chart is 155 stitches wide by 155 stitches high. Mark the outline onto the canvas and make a template (see page 155). If using a white canvas, give it a coat of a watery solution of acrylic to deaden the whiteness. To read the chart, turn the book sideways so that the centre of the book is at the top. Following the chart (see page 154), work the embroidery in tent stitch using *two strands* of tapestry wool together. Work

(Left) *Not working on a frame made the job more portable and quicker to stitch for Julia, but it did distort the flower trellis carpet quite drastically.*

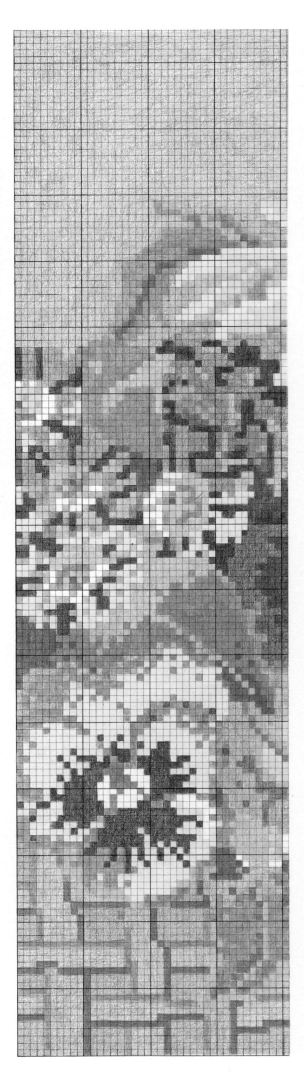

(Above) Detail of
flower trellis carpet.
You can see how the
drawn flower shapes
are being filled in.
The white canvas was
difficult to work
because of the hard
contrast. I would give
the canvas a tint with
an acrylic wash, if
repeating the project.
The cushion is a
section of the carpet,
altered slightly to
make a square
composition.

background (and between lattice) in black
(993). Block the finished needlepoint (see
page 155). Cut and sew the backing (see
page 156). If desired, sew on cord along
seam.

DELFT TABLE MATS

The inspiration for these mats came from a
large Victorian jug (page 120). I first designed a cup from it, which led on to the
mats. The big, bold blooms begged to be
used for needlepoint and translated quite
happily. I also used them on a large scale on
the shaped jug cushion (page 121).

For the first version of the Delft placemat
I tried using off-white and a medium blue
for the centre background. It was quite
good in a softer, less contrasting way than
the final colour scheme with its bright
white. Shades of terracotta or moss-greens
would be interesting alternatives, but blue
and white has a fresh, timeless quality that I
seem to grow fonder of as I get older.
Perhaps this is because I see more and more
exquisite examples of it, from the Orient to
classical Europe. Great tiled buildings in

Portugal are among my favourite blue-and-white compositions. I once painted an entire bathroom to match a large Portuguese panel of tiles, creating the illusion of decorated tiles over every surface, including around the bath and the window and door frames. Even the floor had a blue-and-white border painted on it. The effect was cool and highly decorative. If you are as drawn to the blue-and-white theme as I am, you will find that books on blue-and-white porcelain or tiles provide excellent references.

MATERIALS FOR DELFT TABLE MATS

Rowan DK wool in the following colours and approximate amounts (see page 152):

47 (81m/88yd)	55 (24m/27yd)
49 (40m/44yd)	108 (18m/19yd)
50 (40m/44yd)	☐ 110 (108m/118yd)

10-mesh double-thread or interlocked canvas 48cm/19″ square
45cm/½yd of felt backing fabric
123cm/1¾yd of cord for edging
Finished needlepoint measures approximately 38cm/15″ in diameter.

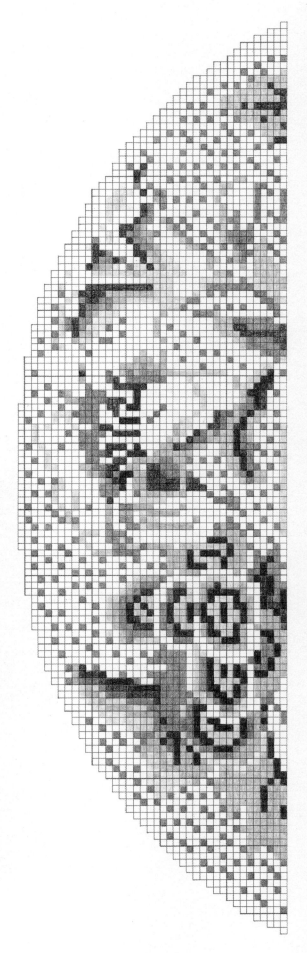

(Right) The toasty golds and browns of this flower pyramid colourway were inspired by marquetry designs.

WORKING DELFT TABLE MAT

The chart is 155 stitches in diameter. Mark the outline onto the canvas and make a template (see page 155). Following the chart (see page 154), work the embroidery in tent stitch using *one strand* of yarn. Block the finished needlepoint (see page 155). Trim canvas edge and along curve, if necessary. Turn back the hem. Cut and sew the backing (see page 156). Sew on cord along seam, tucking ends in beneath backing.

FLOWER PYRAMID CUSHION

This quick, easy-to-stitch cushion is based on a detail from an Oriental carpet. The combination of a classic urn done in two colours and large primitive flowers with bold outlines and centres appealed to me enormously. This is the kind of design you could translate without difficulty into your own personal colour choices. You will see that I have done a version based on mar-quetry-wood tones, but the colours of the bag on page 75 would be elegant. Or, if you like, just change the background to black, to recreate the bold quality of the flower trellis carpet.

When stitching this type of design, I find it easiest to do the outlines first. Then, once I have established the shapes of each flower, I simply fill in the right colours without having to count out the stitches. Do feel free to add more colours to this needlepoint, but to my mind the mirror-image quality is important for the symmetrical flavour of the design. So, if you change the colours on one side of the needlepoint, then echo that same change on the other side most of the time.

Antique carpets are full of good inspiration for needlepoint – the more primitive the better. Just be sure to use enough colour. Even if a carpet only has red, blue and cream in it, the better examples will have many shades of each colour. Tones of yarn that take the dye differently give a richly varied quality that we have to make up for in our needlepoint renderings by using many tones of each colour we choose. Speaking of carpets, repeats of this urn of flowers to create a deep border surrounding a centre of the dotted background would make a gorgeous carpet.

MATERIALS FOR FLOWER PYRAMID CUSHION

Appleton tapestry wool in the following colours and approximate amounts (see page 152):

561 (57m/62yd)   825 (29m/32yd)

693 (32m/35yd)   526 (32m/35yd)
965 (44m/48yd)   251 (17m/19yd)
145 (25m/27yd)   929 (18m/20yd)
947 (30m/33yd)   705 (13m/14yd)
865 (39m/43yd)   503 (22m/24yd)
861 (18m/20yd)   992 (16m/18yd)

■ 744 (30m/33yd) ■ 227 (178m/195yd)
7-mesh double-thread or interlocked canvas 58cm/23" square
1.1m/1¼yd of 90cm/36" fabric and matching thread for ruffle
60cm/¾yd of 90cm/36" backing fabric and matching thread

40cm/16" zip fastener (optional)
Finished needlepoint measures approximately 48cm/19" square.

WORKING FLOWER PYRAMID CUSHION
The chart is 133 stitches wide by 134

■ *(Above) The red lacquer chair and the bright summer blooms make a perfect frame for the lively flower pyramid cushion.*

stitches high. Mark the outline onto the canvas and make a template (see page 155). Following the chart (see page 154), work the embroidery in tent stitch using *two strands* of tapestry wool together. Work background in 227. Block the finished needlepoint (see page 155). For ruffle cut six strips 15cm/6″ wide by 90cm/36″ long and one strip 15cm/6″ by 45cm/18″. Sew strips together end-to-end to form a circle, press seams and fold in half lengthwise, wrong sides together. Sew ruffle to needlepoint (see page 156). Cut and sew the backing (see page 156).

TRICIA'S BASKET CHAIRS

Years ago, I designed my first collection of furnishing fabrics for Tricia Guild at her King's Road shop. I used bouquets of flowers and overlapping geranium leaves as themes. To top off the collection she wanted two old basket chairs done in needlepoint. I did one of my big bouquets of flowers and leaves (including the striped geranium leaves) surrounding a wicker lattice on a dull pink ground. I wanted to have the prettiness of flowers, on a base of tweedy-looking wicker and dull pink, to harmonize with the antique chairs.

The chair seat is reproduced here as a cushion. You should be able to do similar arrangements yourself, after studying this very simplistic approach to leaves and flowers. Any strongly patterned flowers or

■ *(Below) Detail of seat of basket chair.*

■ *(Right) The basket chairs tone well with the old crocks, the soft rubbed walls and the terracotta floor of Tricia's kitchen. Richard Womersley blankets cover the arms of each chair.*

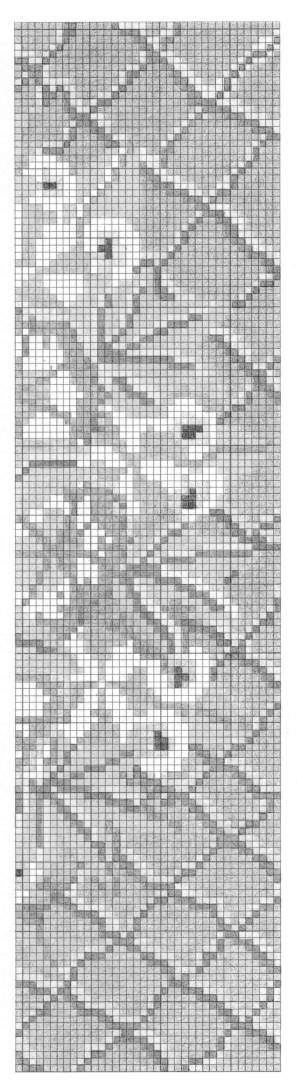

leaves would lend themselves to this simplified treatment.

MATERIALS FOR BOUQUET CUSHION

Appleton tapestry wool in the following colours and approximate amounts (see page 152):

■ 145 (6m/6½yd)	▓ 874 (16m/18yd)
■ 755 (19m/21yd)	▒ 251a (24m/26yd)
▓ 751 (41m/45yd)	▓ 242 (21m/23yd)
▓ 953 (63m/69yd)	▓ 293 (22m/24yd)
■ 956 (6m/6½yd)	▒ 841 (35m/39yd)
▒ 987 (63m/69yd)	□ 992 (133m/145yd)
▒ 474 (18m/19yd)	▓ 693 (43m/47yd)
▓ 861 (28m/31yd)	▓ 942 (9m/10yd)
▓ 562 (37m/40yd)	▓ 142 (133m/145yd)

7-mesh double-thread or interlocked canvas 63cm/25" by 64cm/25½"
60cm/¾yd of 90cm/36" backing fabric and matching thread
2.2m/2½yd of cord (optional)
46cm/18" zip fastener (optional)
Finished needlepoint measures approximately 53cm/21" by 54cm/21½".

WORKING BOUQUET CUSHION

The chart is 147 stitches wide by 151 stitches high. Mark the outline onto the canvas and make a template (see page 155). Following the chart (see page 154), work the embroidery in tent stitch using *two strands* of tapestry wool together. Block the finished needlepoint (see page 155). Cut and sew backing (see page 156). Sew on cord.

■ *(Left) The bouquet cushion is based on the seat of Tricia's basket chairs.*

*(Previous page)
The tulip bench
covering was inspired
by its marquetry back.
My drawing of a tulip
and the bench are
inset into the long-
stitch seat of the
bench.*

*(Below) When I
am working on
something like the
flower shoulder bag, I
like to see how
similarly coloured
objects harmonize.
This beautifully faded
umbrella, painted
bucket and lavender
bush give the bag a
mellow glow.*

*(Far right) The
flower shoulder bag.*

TULIP TAPESTRY

A client presented me with this marquetry bench she had found and commissioned a needlepoint covering. The marquetry bench inspired my row of flowers which adorn its seat. Stitching the tulips against a landscape of old map forms gave the seat a warm, airy feeling. The first sample I attempted came out too dark and heavy so I chose a higher, lighter palette. Even though the flowers look complex their structure is very simple, with dark to lightest shading on each section. The deep rusts and maroons of the flowers toned well with the wood.

FLOWER SHOULDER BAG

It is plain to see that I lifted the idea for this shoulder bag from a Middle Eastern saddle bag. The rows of almost identical flowers appeal to me. I like repetition, if done in a loose, varied way. Often very carefully matched repeated forms make for a mechanically rigid design.

The strap handle of the bag has a very symmetrical pattern shape, but the colours change it enough to save it from getting too predictable. This strap could have many applications. It could be made into a cap by working a piece long enough to fit around your head and adding a circular centre of dark velvet or other fabric. Or it could be worked as a belt lined with thin leather or linen fabric. I can also see it, bordering a continuous row of the flowers, as handsome braiding on heavy curtains.

MATERIALS FOR FLOWER SHOULDER BAG

Rowan DK wool in the following colours and approximate amounts (see page 152):

	410 (37m/41yd)		416 (66m/75yd)
	93 (34m/38yd)		605 (87m/96yd)
	94 (67m/74yd)		418 (54m/60yd)
	82 (61m/68yd)		88 (49m/54yd)
	616 (115m/127yd)		54 (42m/47yd)
	59 (15m/16yd)		3 (3m/3yd)
	109 (12m/13yd)		407 (230m/256yd)
	27 (57m/63yd)		

10-mesh double-thread or interlocked canvas 78cm/31″ by 114cm/45″
140cm/1½yd of 90cm/36″ lining fabric and matching thread
Finished needlepoint front or back measures approximately 39cm/15½″ square, strap approximately 4.5cm/1¾″ by 163cm/64″ and bottom approximately 4.5cm/1¾″ by 39cm/15½″.

WORKING FLOWER SHOULDER BAG

The bag is worked in four pieces: front, back, strap and bottom. The chart for the front or back is 155 stitches wide by 154 stitches high. The chart for the strap is 18 stitches wide and 155 stitches long and is repeated lengthwise until the strap is approximately 163cm/64″ long. (Note: The strap forms the sides of the bag.) The bottom is 18 stitches wide by 155 stitches long. Mark the outlines for the front, back, strap and bottom onto the canvas and make templates (see page 155). Following the chart (see

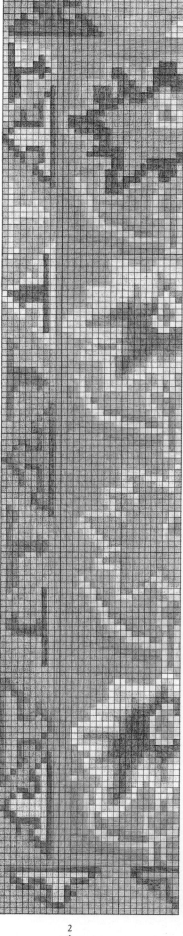

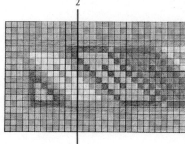

(Right) *The flower shoulder bag was inspired by Caucasian carpets.*

76

3　1

3　1

page 154), work the embroidery for the first side in tent stitch using *one strand* of yarn. Work the second side in the same way. To read the strap chart, turn the book sideways so that the centre of the page is at the bottom. Following the chart, work the embroidery until line 1 is reached, then begin again from line 2. Continue repeating

the chart in this way until the strap measures 162cm/63¾″ or desired length, then finish with a border of the little squares over an extra three rows of stitches. For the bottom of the bag work the chart from the beginning to line 3, then finish with a border of the little squares. Block the finished needlepoints (see page 155). Cut pieces of lining the same sizes as front,

back, strap and bottom plus a 1.5cm/⅝″ seam allowance. With right sides of lining facing, sew bottom to back and front, then sew strap to back and front along sides. Trim canvas to 1cm/½″ around needlepoint pieces. Fold the canvas edge back all around and join all the pieces as for the lining, but with the wrong sides facing and working a

half cross-stitch seam with 407 (see page 155). Insert lining into bag. Turn under hems of lining and needlepoint along top edges of bag and along strap. Stitch lining to needlepoint with an invisible seam.

BARGELLO FLOWER BENCH

One of the joys of having a bit of a track record in the needlepoint field is getting commissions like this one. Victoria Weymouth brought me fabrics and the dimensions of a bench required for a house she was decorating. Left to my own devices, I sought out bold fantasy flowers from English fabrics and drew my versions of them out on the right-sized paper. I traced these onto canvas and started stitching away, keeping her fabric samples nearby to get the colour balance right. I used a mock bargello-stitch background with random colours that changed often. As I started doing the background in the wrong direction, I decided to keep it like this, making the flowers stand out better with the difference in stitch direction. This is the sort of project that lends itself to group stitching. I had three students helping me on it and, once a flower was established or a background series of colours put in, it could be completed by anyone who had a bit of a feel for the random quality of the work. I can think of few more enjoyable ways of spending time with people than working together to create a colourful textile.

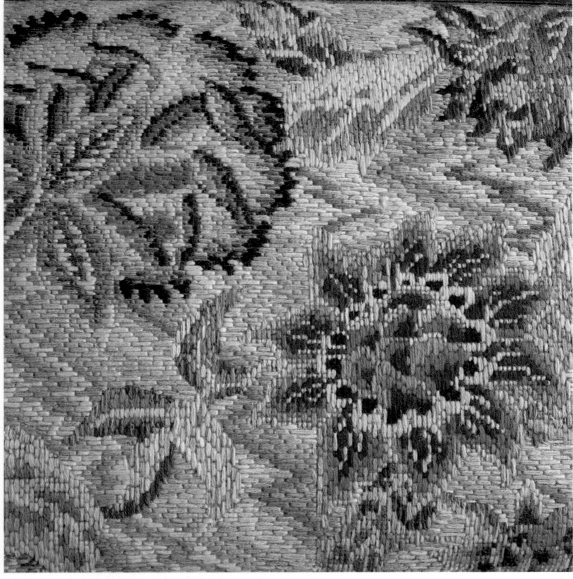

■ *(Left and below)*
More details of the
bargello flower bench.

■ (Right) Note how the flat areas of single colour are contrasted with the mottled, mixed-thread areas.

■ (Below) The finished tropical floral chair.

■ (Opposite page) The tropical floral chair is shown here in progress with a friend's gorgeous collection of painted Kashmiri boxes and tables.

TROPICAL FLORAL CHAIR

The interesting thing about this work is that it grew completely organically – no colour sketches were done. After doing a large outline drawing in waterproof pen on the canvas, I stitched in one leaf at a time. As I stitched the large areas of colour, I began to add 'washes' of colour by mixing my yarns. As this was all done in double threads, it was easy to have each strand a different colour – keeping the main colour going, but changing its partner from tone to tone. This created a subtle ripple of colour.

I chose a bold, cheerful, Matisse-like colourway with mysterious undertones to marry the work to the old wood of the chair.

The flowers, inspired by old embroideries and Chinese pot decorations, are set against a jungle of cloud-like leaves. The tobacco and deep rusts tone with the wood. The main task here was to keep the outlines as contrasting as possible without making them so sharp that they would jump out of the complex of colours. I worked the outlines first to get good, crisp shapes on pointed veins or scallops. After softening most of the seat colours, I dropped in a high royal blue shaded to a pale sky in one of the flowers. This seems to make all the colours dance a bit.

You will notice that most areas of colour are broken up with subtle shadings. Occasionally an outlined vein or part of a leaf is done in a solid colour, followed by shadings that seem to give more movement to the leaves.

GARDEN TAPESTRY COUCH

Of all the commissions I have had so far this was the most challenging and successful. The brief was to cover a modern couch below an old tapestry in a way that harmonized with it. I immediately perceived the idea of continuing the scene in the tapestry down over the couch surface to the floor. The trick was to keep the colours as

muted- and aged-looking as the tapestry had become over the years. I drew out a rough watercolour in my sketch book. Then I did a final drawing, having the water flow from my new pool over the edge to echo the

(Above) Details of autumn landscape tapestry.

(Opposite page) Completed tapestry.

with an atmospheric needlepoint covering. This is, of course, particularly successful when it echoes other furnishings in a room, such as a fireplace or carpet or, in this case, a tapestry.

AUTUMN LANDSCAPE TAPESTRY

The thrilling thing about doing textiles as a living is to get commissions like this tapestry. I was asked by Hugh Ehrman's mother to do a tapestry to go in her newly converted, old Cotswold home. The entrance hall had two handsome Oriental bowls that inspired the focal point in my tapestry. For the rest, I looked at lots of Japanese prints and paintings, observing how simplistic a lot of their grasses and leaves were. I drew the outlines of grasses and leaves and shoreline and started stitching variations of pastel tones. I was careful to keep it all fairly light in tone, even in shadow areas. I used white silk for the porcelain on the pot, giving only the merest hint of shading. The shading in the water and sky was achieved by changing colours very gradually (see page 154).

This is the type of commission that is ideal for long stitch. Using double yarn on 7-mesh canvas, the work grows quickly and creates a good, flexible fabric which hangs well.

CAUCASIAN FLOWER CUSHION

I include this cushion because it still pleases me years after designing it and was the first needlepoint design that started my long association with Ehrman's. It is amazing to us all that after a number of years it is still going strong in Ehrman's catalogue.

The inspiration came from carpets and the highly painted trucks of Afghanistan. When I first went to that beautiful country years ago, I was thunderstruck by the joyful decorations on buses, wagons and trucks. The idea of these tough workmen having their vehicles decorated with flowers, birds, landscapes, even jet planes and trains totally caught my imagination.

The flowers and vase are from a carpet idea, but the layout and corner details are from stencil motifs used on the trucks.

Steve's arrangement with all those sumptuous shades of pink and the soft colouring

fountain above. I drew onto the canvas of the eight cushions and the long running base board. I was late starting, so pushed myself night and day and got it all done in a little over two weeks with one other helper. It is exciting to see what you can achieve when up against it – with the help of long stitch and 7-mesh canvas! The stitching is only on the surfaces that show. Brown felt lines the underside and back edges of the cushions.

The finished couch is proof that the hard lines of a modern couch can be softened

■ *(Right) My first concept sketch for the Caucasian flower and the finished artwork for the needlepoint kit.*

■ *(Far right) The jug with its pastel fan and the high flower colours really bring to life the Caucasian flower cushion.*

of the china should give you plenty of ideas for further versions of this concept. It is shot at Tricia Guild's London house where her Victorian jug so perfectly echoes our colours.

This bringing together of colour schemes in various objects is one of the most enjoyable aspects of needlepoint. Think of the fun you can have reproducing colours of your favourite pots, carpets, or other furnishings in needlepoint designs to make a cohesive colour scheme.

FACES AND FANS

THE face is a powerful image. Being a constant source of emotional expression, it never fails to fascinate us. A still face contains great mystery and faces have been used with beautiful dramatic effect on all sorts of patterned surfaces. Fans, boxes, door frames and classic Toby jugs are just a few decorative uses the face has been put to.

Many sources for face designs spring vividly to my mind. Masks and theatrical make-up, such as clowns, Kabuki or Peking Opera faces, create bold effects. The natives of so-called 'primitive' worlds play with striking face painting and decorated masks that are also excellent subjects. The theatrical Victorian masks on page 56 have wonderful colourings for needlepoint projects. I can see them overlapping on a large easy chair, or separately as cushions. English enamelled snuff boxes in the shape of faces are an excellent source.

For this book I've chosen the stark white

■ *(Left) Steve's explosion of overlapping fans really celebrates their jaunty shapes. Some of the faces are watercolours I did on blank paper fans. Note the fan-encrusted jug.*

■ *(Below) My sketches of Mexican masks from the Museum of Mankind in London.*

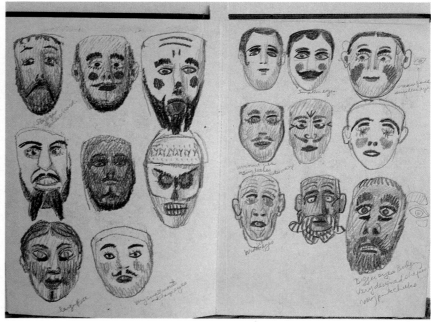

FACES AND FANS

■ (*Previous page*) *The chalky white of the Kabuki face is right at home with this Chinese red silk and bright pink plaid. It would be equally exciting in a very stark contemporary setting.*

■ (*Right*) *Here we see the Kabuki inspiration photo on top of my template watercolour and the half-stitched canvas. After doing the shaded areas, I was able to quickly fill in solid white rows.*

92

of the Kabuki face, the weathered stone surface of a colossus' head, and the nostalgia of the Victorian era in the children's and cats' faces. Many other animals could be used for equally good results – such as dogs, monkeys, lions.

Fans, with their bold graceful arcs, have decorated many an object in the West and especially the East. The idea of doing a chapter on faces and fans came from seeing a mask fan made from a Hogarth design of 1728. A pale, moon-like face sits boldly in the middle of an intricately painted fan. The radiating fan folds make a mysterious distortion to the images painted on them, or serve as decoration in themselves. I have used just simple stripes on the fans for the lampshade on page 117, letting the folds alone create the pattern.

KABUKI

I was struck by the realistic eyes peering out of the paper white Kabuki flat face. As you can see from the in-progress shot, I did the eyes, nose and mouth first, then the side shadings, and filled in the remainder with solid white. Leaving a few stitches out at the mouth opening created a realistic shadow. We have photographed this Kabuki face in a romantic, Oriental setting, but I really thought of it as the one detailed piece in an austere hi-tech environment – all black-and-white, perhaps. You could take other, more dramatic, Oriental theatre faces for even bolder effects. These could be done with rudimentary flat shapes, not needing the skill for shading in order to define the face. Clown faces, too, would make good needle-points. I like Victorian and earlier styles of make-up. The Chinese opera faces, for instance, with large, blushing cheeks would make very cheery cushions.

MATERIALS FOR KABUKI FACE CUSHION

Appleton tapestry wool in the following colours and approximate amounts (see page 152):

184 (one skein)		766 (one skein)	
187 (one skein)		964 (one skein)	
304 (one skein)		993 (one skein)	
751 (one skein)		992 (one skein)	
757 (one skein)		991 (208m/231yd)	

One skein each of the following Appleton crewel wools for mixing shades:

223	941	
292	942	
501	944	
521	945	
642	961	
702	962	
708	963	
914	967	
915	970	
991	972	
992	974	

10-mesh double-thread linen canvas 45cm/18″ by 46cm/18½″
1m/1yd of 90cm/36″ backing fabric and matching thread
35cm/½yd of 90cm/36″ fabric in red and purple for mitred frame
1.5m/1¾yd of piping cord
30cm/12″ zip fastener (optional)
Finished needlepoint measures approximately 35cm/14″ by 36cm/14½″.

COLOUR MIXTURES

Where there is only one colour number, use either *one strand* of tapestry wool or *three strands* of crewel wool. Where there are two or more colour numbers, use *three strands* of crewel.

A = 993; B = 991; C = 766; D = 304; E = 187; F = 2 strands of 914 and 1 of 915; G = 2 strands of 708 and 1 of 223; H = 751; I = 941; J = 961; K = 757; L = 2 strands of 223 and 1 of 941; M = 963; N = 2 strands of 991 and 1 of 961; O = 1 strand each 961, 708 and 991; P = 2 strands of 945 and 1 of 501; Q = 2 strands of 945 and 1 of 942; R = 2 strands of 942 and 1 of 945; S = 2 strands of 942 and 1 of 702; T = 2 strands of 944 and 1 of 501; U = 1 strand each 945, 501 and 223; Z = 964; AA = 2 strands of 944 and 1 of 945; BB = 2 strands of 501 and 1 of 945; CC = 184; DD = 2 strands of 972 and 1 of 642; EE = 1 strand each 961, 972 and 642; FF = 1 strand each 991, 972 and 642; GG = 2 strands of 961 and 1 of 521; HH = 2 strands of 521 and 1 of 702; JJ = 2 strands of 961 and 1 of 991; KK = 992; LL = 2 strands of 991 and 1 of 708.

WORKING KABUKI FACE CUSHION

This needlepoint is for the more adventur-

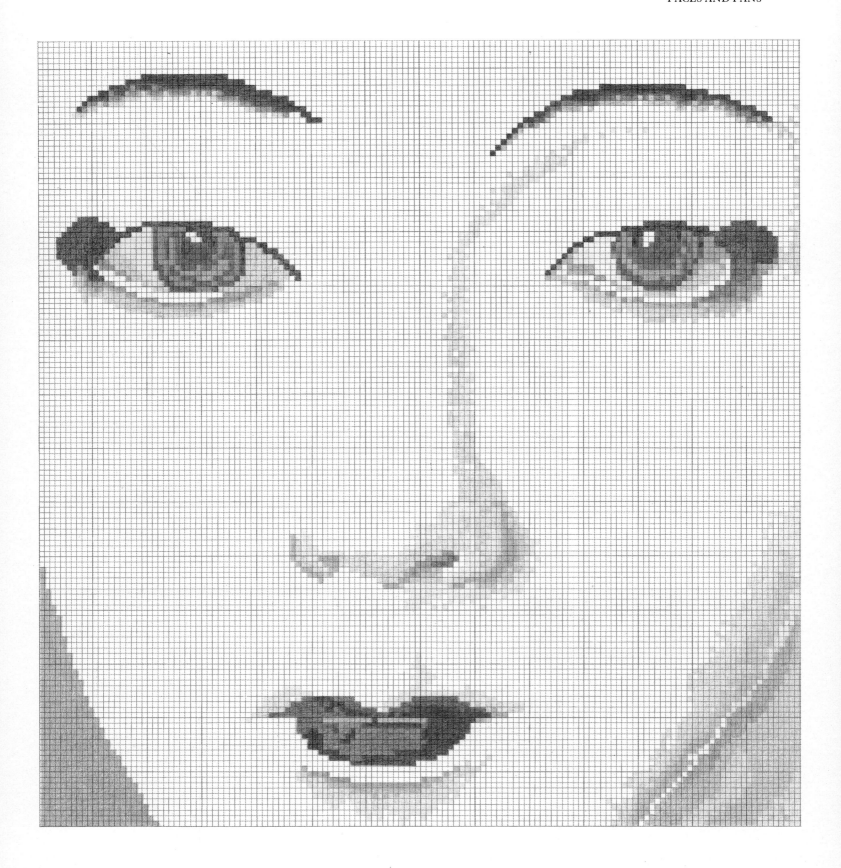

■ *(Right) This elegantly restrained room makes a perfect home for the stone head cushion.*

■ *(Below) In-progress shot of stone head, photographed in a London cemetery.*

■ *(Opposite page) The detail of the stone head shows the strands of mixed colours used to create subtle transitions in tone.*

ous embroiderer who wants to try out toning and shading effects (see page 154). Follow the colour key above for mixing the various tones and shades. Only where one colour number has been used will the colour on the chart match the coloured squares in the materials section. The chart is 140 stitches wide by 145 stitches high. Mark the outline onto the canvas and make a template (see page 155). Following the chart as a guide (see page 154), work the embroidery

in tent stitch in the following order, shading and toning with the colours indicated:

Eyelashes – **A**. *Pupils* – **A**, **B** and **E**. *Irises* – Outline with **E** and shade with **F**, **D** and **C**. *Whites of eyes* – Left eye: **N** and **O**. Right eye: **N**, **O** and **DD**. *Eye make-up circles* – Left eye: **P**. Right eye: **P**, **K** and **R**. *Line for lower lid* – **B** and **G**. *Shading under eye* – Left eye: **I**, **H** and **LL**. Right eye: **I**, **H**, **O**, **LL**, **L**, **M**, and **J**. *Eyebrows* – Left: **BB**, **Q**, **R**, and **S**. Right: **P**, **AA** and **R**. *Lips* – Leave a line of plain canvas for the centre of the mouth. Upper lip: **U**, **Q** and **K**. Lower lip: **U**, **P**, **Q** and **T**. Shade face for a few stitches above top lip with **GG**, **JJ** and **KK**. *Indent above chin* – **EE**, **GG**, **JJ** and **KK**. *Nostrils* – **F**, **CC**, **DD**, **FF**, **GG**, **JJ** and **KK**. *Bridge of nose* – **HH**, **JJ** and **KK**. *Left side of face* – **Z**. *Right side of face* – Use mixtures of the following crewel yarns to create shadings here: 292, 521, 642, 961, 962, 963, 967, 970, 974 and 992. *Remainder of face* – **B**.

Block the finished needlepoint (see page 155). Cut four strips of red fabric 8cm/3¼" wide and 51cm/20" long, and four strips of purple fabric 6cm/2¼" wide and 56cm/22" long. Sew the mitred frame, backing and piping (see pages 156 and 157).

STONE HEAD

For this colossus' head – seen in an article in the Italian magazine *FMR* – I have used a range of very close tones. The powerful drama of the source picture greatly inspired me. Those deep-shadowed eye sockets and great atmospheric streaks were elements that really defined the face. I used about fifteen actual colours, but many of them were combinations of crewel threads – ochre and cream together, or grey and brown to give a grainy texture to the shadows and rain streaks. I followed the photograph of the stone head as closely as possible, but did not mind if I veered from it in tone, and it seemed to be working. Stone textures and colours can be wonderful as furnishings, as they are very easy to live with and will not date like other highly coloured objects sometimes do. It was my intention to do a bower of carved stone flowers in needle-point as a border for a doorway. I did not

(*Previous page*) *Here are the results of my attraction to Victorian scraps of these big-eyed cats. The bold lace makes a chunky border.*

(*Right*) *Just a few of the 2,500 needlepoint pictures people sent in for the Heritage tapestry.*

(*Below*) *I love the way these guys settle snugly into this Collier Campbell chintz.*

(*Opposite page*) *My cat sketches and design sources, and more charming squares from the Heritage tapestry. Dogs and cats were just two of the dozens of themes that poured through my letterbox after my TV appeal.*

have time to complete that for this book, but I pass the concept on to you.

If, like me, you are attracted to antique furnishings and a faded, muted colour scheme, this stone look would be a harmonious addition to your house. The tapestry couch on page 82 is a good example of harmonizing with existing antique furnishings.

CATS

I have gone for a deliberately pretty effect for these cats. It projects a rather kitsch, Victorian look with the pink bow and lace edge, but I tried to get a gutsiness into their handsome markings and huge, wild eyes. I used many mixtures of crewel-thread colours to produce shadings in the fur. The 7-mesh canvas made it possible to use five different colours of crewel at a time. The exciting thing about highly varied surfaces like fur is having the freedom to improvise while observing the source material. You can take chances, exaggerate colours, and still come up with effects that are quite life-like. I work very quickly, so I do not think

too much about the exact colours. Rather than slavishly producing a photo-image, I try to capture the feel of my subject. The very size of the canvas and huge stitches have a stylized effect, anyway. The lace border was easy to achieve. I just took a reference from a lace book, drew it out and stitched it in off-white with a dark-grey ground for contrast. Unfortunately, it was impossible to make a kit for my cat needle-point, or to include a chart for it here. There were just too many mixtures of colours involved. The large reproduction should enable you to copy it pretty closely, if you wish. There are about five ochery golds, six mid-browns, four dark browns, seven pink and peach tones, three greens, four blues and about four greys; a lavender and rust in small areas complete the line-up. These basic colours are infinitely expanded by being used doubly or in groups of five, when crewel weight is employed.

There are many excellent books on the market depicting cats in art and photography, so you are spoiled for choice if looking for your own source. Black-and-white or

(Below) The patch Buddha can be made as a cutout-shaped cushion or with a little multi-toned cloud background.

tortoise-shell cats would be a gift to a beginner – the bold placement of colour patches alone always looks like a cat, even with primitive distortions.

BUDDHA CUSHIONS

The image of the porcelain Buddha with its bold patchwork robe has always thrilled me since I first visited the Victoria and Albert Museum twenty-two years ago. Many of the highly decorated Oriental porcelains in this museum would make excellent subjects – such as the yellow dragon vase (page 103), which I sketched in the Seventies to use as a needlepoint. The laughing Buddha with his high pastel colours and dark blood-red has

lots of white front lines in scales
and clowds
little scales dark blue
large bellie ones pale blue

little curly clowds on vase
(very articulated
bein line curls)

White edge
on robe braidi

■ *(Previous page) This particular version of the Buddha (see source below right) in vivid patches is one of my favourite displays at the Victoria and Albert Museum. I did this sketch soon after arriving in London in the late Sixties.*

■ *(Right) I first encountered the laughing Buddha in San Francisco's Chinatown when I was a small boy. I later included him in a still life. His bright pastels and rotund whiteness still cheer me up, so stitching him was good fun.*

been a friend since I bought him in San Francisco's Chinatown in the Sixties. I have often painted him in my still lifes, and had fun stitching him and his adoring throng on 7-mesh canvas.

MATERIALS FOR BUDDHA CUSHION
Appleton tapestry wool in the following colours and approximate amounts (see page 152):

▨	553 (69m/76yd)	▨	947 (31m/34yd)
▨	525 (17m/19yd)	▨	886 (49m/54yd)
▨	463 (53m/58yd)	▨	963 (21m/23yd)
▨	749 (21m/23yd)	▨	875 (38m/42yd)
▨	752 (35m/38yd)	☐	991b (93m/102yd)
▨	251a (34m/37yd)		872 (107m/117yd)

10-mesh double-thread or interlocked canvas 60cm/24" square
60cm/¾yd of 90cm/36" backing fabric and matching thread
2.1m/2½yd of cord for edging
41cm/16" zip fastener (optional)
Finished needlepoint is about 50cm/20" square.

WORKING SQUARE BUDDHA CUSHION
The finished needlepoint cushion is 199 stitches wide by 200 stitches high. (Note: The chart is 149 stitches wide by 191 stitches high. See below for extending background.) Mark outline onto the canvas and make a template (see page 155). Following the chart (see page 154), work the embroidery in tent stitch using *one strand* of tapestry wool. Work background in 872. Extend background, using 872 and adding 2 rows at bottom, 7 rows at top, 26 rows at right-hand edge and 24 rows at left-hand edge. Repeat cloud motifs into extended background as

Reprinted from
A History of Printed Scraps
New Cavendish Books
ISBN 0 904568 29 3

MADE IN ENGLAND

A2

(Previous page) Boy and girl needlepoints in progress with sources.

(Right) In-progress shot of the boy cushion with the Victorian scrap that inspired it.

(Opposite page) Completed boy and girl cushions in a South London garden.

desired. Block the finished needlepoint (see page 155). Cut and sew the backing (see page 156). Sew on cord along seam.

For shaped Buddha cushion, work as for square Buddha cushion, but embroider only to edge of Buddha figure and throne, omitting all background in 872.

CHILD'S HEAD

What attracted me to these printed scraps of Victorian heads was the colours of their outfits and rich variety of tones in their hair. The hats, particularly, were wonderful to stitch with the ochre chestnut-browns and range of dull blues. I think the vague touches of gold decoration done in muted yellow-ochres came out well. Steve's idea to do these heads as cut-out shapes has resulted in doll-like cushions. I have used masses of colours, particularly in the girl's head, and many double-crewel combinations for shading. The beauty of working with these crewel threads is the ability to use quite unexpected colours in the hair and flesh, by keeping one thread of flesh tone while the second thread in the needle can be pale-blue, green or lavender, and the whole face still hangs together. You will notice a quite daring pale green-blue shadow on the girl's forehead.

On the boy, the colours are more restrained – creams and shades of blue, with ochre-gold decoration. The trick here was to have enough variety and shading to break up the areas of colour, without going too wild and losing the soft innocent colours of the Victorian cut-out. Sometimes, for a certain kind of drama one wants large, flat areas of one colour, but I usually try to break up areas of colour with shading and ripples of 'painted' tone. Of course, a real doll done in needlepoint would be delicious.

I backed the shaped heads with a grey, pin-stripe wool, but for a doll you could work needlepoint hair, etc. for the back. I was going to do a doll myself for this book, but time and deadlines put paid to that. Do try it for yourself. Even a teddy bear with its shades of fur would be wonderful in needle-point.

MOSAIC HEAD PLATE

London's Portobello Flea Market was a river of magic objects to my 'fresh-from-California' eyes. In 1965 I had the good luck to find a large room four streets away from the market. I spent every weekend sifting through piles of old fabrics, china and decorative goodies from all over the world. This mosaic was typical of the stimulating things you could pick up for a song in those days. It figured in some of my early still lifes and became the subject for my third needle-point project. The stitching took forever, as it was done on 12-mesh canvas. But some-thing like a mosaic proved a great stretch for me, playing with the little fragments of different types of pattern – especially the coronation portrait. A mosaic pattern would be excellent for things like lamp bases or -shades, waste baskets or a mad tea cosy.

I first did a watercolour of the plate to familiarize myself with the separate patterns on the broken china pieces. Then I drew on my canvas and got started. The deep-khaki ground contrasted well with the sharp, paler china. For the corners of my square I played with many geometric stitches (one of the few times I ever have). If this mosaic reminds you that fragments of patterned china are delightful, why not find a book on Gaudi's mosaic bench in Barcelona. Or better still go to Spain to see it! Its long serpentine form is studded with bright pieces of boldly decorated tiles and crock-ery. Mosaic can have many distinctly differ-ent moods like its fabric counterpart, patch-work: all pastel colours, for instance, or mostly creams and plain white with the odd colourful pattern dropped in here and there; for a deep, rich effect, many bright, solid colours on a dark ground, or quite a modern feeling from just striped china pieces going in different directions. My all-time favour-ites are the classic blue-and-white mosaics. The one that Steve has constructed (page 121) is just one of the many moods to be achieved. You can go from heavy, bold markings for drama to the most delicate effect, mostly white with a few fragile blue patterns, for a fresh, light feeling. Then there are mixtures of colours and blue and

(Below) To get the scale right for the needlepoint opposite, I first painted a watercolour sketch twice the size of the mosaic plate from Portobello Market.

(Opposite page) The fineness of the canvas gives a good sharp, detailed look, but is quite time-consuming.

■ (*Right*) *Steve made a marvellously theatrical arrangement for the fan throw with two of my paintings and everything toasty-toned we could lay our hands on.*

white – such as a table I have that is primrose-yellow pieces with many old willow-pattern bits. To experiment before stitching, cut out pieces of patterned paper and make a collage mosaic as a sketch. You could make a very amusing chair or couch covered in mosaic needlepoint – in larger stitches, of course!

FAN THROW

This piece could be called the story of a kimono, a clay pot, two fans and a parasol, for these are the varied sources that fill my jaunty fans. I have always loved fans, especially when they overlap in a lively design such as one sees so inventively done on the lacquer boxes, embroidered kimonos, patterned papers and porcelains of Japan.

Once I had decided on the designs and colouring for the fans, it was just a matter of choosing a ground that would suit them all. I finally settled on the tawny warmth of mellow-gold into rust, which had such a glowing feeling. I divided the background with a roughly drawn lattice which I picked out in a lighter gold. I like the contrast

(Below) The sources for the fan throw were two fans, a china pot, a cotton parasol and a detail of a painted kimono.

(Right) The fan throw gives just a taste of the painterly qualities long stitch is capable of producing.

between the watercolour wash of the iris fan (copied from one in the Victoria and Albert Museum in London) and the paper cut-out feel of the morning glory one beside it. The fresh blue-and-cream plaid and nasturtium came from an old cloth parasol. The stylized poppies on their black cloud-like ground decorated a handsome Japanese pot, and the large red peony I found on a hand-painted kimono. Though roughly 1m/3ft square, it moved along at a lovely clip, as it was done in long stitch on 7-mesh canvas. I can see it used to brighten up the back of a couch or thrown over a trunk.

FAN LAMPSHADE

Most of the designs in this book are what some would regard as 'busy' – certainly detailed over every inch of their surfaces. Sometimes one requires a bold, crisp simplicity with just a hint of decoration. To show the folding shape of these fans I have done a simple two-tone effect, with a coloured stripe or two running through each one. This folding-fan illusion is easy to achieve, and adding just a touch of variation to the shadow areas makes them quite convincing. I also lightened the gun-metal grey towards the centre of the shade. I used three crewel threads in long stitch on 10-mesh canvas. Actually, there are places where the canvas shows through, so four strands of crewel may be needed to really cover it. I rather like the linen colour of the canvas showing in some of my work, particularly with old shell colours or in certain landscapes. Fan cushions echoing whatever colour you have in your room would be easy to achieve.

(Below) On the fan lampshade before mounting you can see the softening of the grey ground towards the centre and slight changes of tone in fan colours.

(Right) I painted the base of the fan lampshade in acrylics, using the old, stained water jug as a model. One of my early still lifes is behind the lamp.

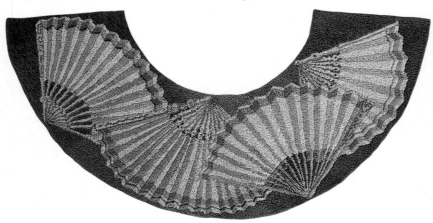

JUGS AND GEOMETRICS

JUGS, pots and china of all kinds have always attracted my attention when looking for designs. My mother and grandmother sowed the seeds of this attraction by collecting handsome Italian, Dutch and, especially, Oriental pots. When I arrived in England and fell upon the Portobello Flea Market and all its wondrous shops filled with a gypsy's dream of decorated china, I was in heaven. The borders, floral motifs, bold and delicate colours all found their way into my still lifes first, knitting and needlepoint later. I haunted the Victoria and Albert Museum in London doing watercolours of my favourite china pieces. Figurative elements, like flowers and animals or houses, attracted me at first but, more and more, I began to apply the abstract use of geometrics to my textile work as a vehicle for colour.

Geometrics or textural patterns are a natural for anyone interested in colourful textiles. You can quickly memorize most patterns and concentrate on your own personal arrangement of colour. Diagonal stripes, plaids, tumbling blocks, circles, steps – all can become unique, if the colours come from your heart.

JUG-SHAPED CUSHIONS
The green-and-lavender jug is a favourite of Antoinette Allsopp's. She has focused our attention on these Staffordshire jugs by making such a splendid collection of them in her shop, Putnam's, in North London. The blue-and-white jug has been a faithful friend to me, feeding me inspiration for paintings, mugs, placemats (page 61) and tapestries. The poor thing is broken in a dozen places, but is glued together and still adorns my shelves. Its big boldness was quite easy to portray in this long-stitch cushion on 7-mesh canvas. I used off-white on it, but bright white on the green-and-lavender jug, where the background is done in tent stitch to depict the little geometric pattern.

BLUE-AND-WHITE POT CUSHION
Blue and white on china increases in beauty and freshness as one gets older. Most deco-

■ (Opposite page) Blue-and-white jugs set against my still-life painting.

■ (Far left) Sketch for my Oriental arrangement tapestry on page 9.

■ (Left) Sketch from my notebook of a jug in the Victoria and Albert Museum.

rative traditions around the world have rich histories of blue-and-white designs on chinaware and tiles. The Scandinavians, the Portuguese, the Russians, the English and particularly the Dutch, with their famously witty tiles, have fed me many a good textile idea. But the Orient, from Turkey to China and Japan, has been the most direct of my influences.

The blue-and-white pot cushion is an amalgam of sources. The shape came from a book on Chinese porcelain. The actual pattern you can see in my in-progress shot is from an English bowl copied from the Chinese in 1780. The flowers on the background come from the old beaded purse. It is so easy to translate bead work to tent stitch, bead for stitch! The yellow was inspired by my delight at Monet's yellow kitchen which made such a good background for his rows of blue-and-white plates.

■ *(Below) My painting of blue-and-white china.*

■ *(Right) These jug-shaped cushions in long stitch could strike an amusing note in a china collector's interior. A mosaic version in needlepoint would be even more witty.*

MATERIALS FOR BLUE-AND-WHITE POT CUSHION

Appleton tapestry wool in the following colours and approximate amounts (see page 152):

■ 461 (38m/42yd)		■ 947 (4.5m/5yd)	
■ 744 (64m/69yd)		■ 754 (18m/19yd)	
■ 823 (47m/52yd)		■ 751 (40m/44yd)	
□ 992 (123m/134yd)		■ 431 (14m/15yd)	
■ 551 (121m/133yd)		■ 526 (14m/15yd)	

10-mesh double-thread or interlocked

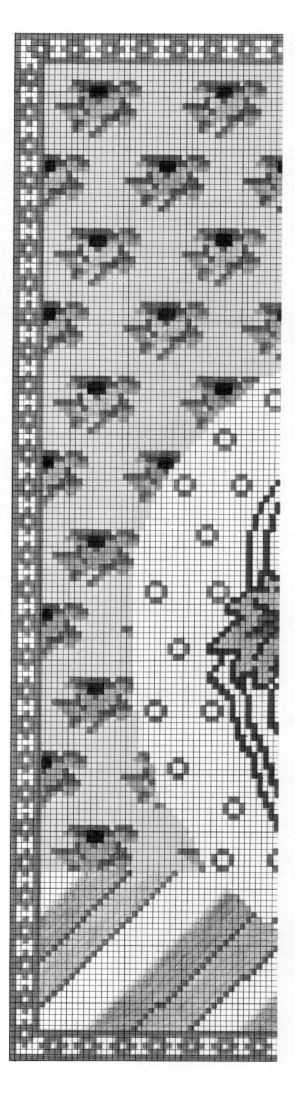

(*Previous page*) *Blue-and-white pot and bowl cushions in an English summer garden.*

(*Above*) *Here are the sources for the blue-and-white pot tapestry. The little beaded bag gave me the repeated rose motif for the background and the bowl gave me the basket of flowers.*

canvas 55cm/22″ square
1m/1¼yd of 90cm/36″ fabric and matching thread for ruffle
60cm/¾yd of 90cm/36″ backing fabric and matching thread
36cm/14″ zip fastener (optional)
Finished needlepoint measures aproximately 45cm/18″ square.

WORKING BLUE-AND-WHITE POT CUSHION

The chart is 180 stitches wide by 180 stitches high. Mark the outline onto the canvas and make a template (see page 155). Following the chart (see page 154), work the embroidery in tent stitch using *one strand* of tapestry wool. For a sharper contrast, substitute white (991) for off-white (992). Block the finished needlepoint (see page 155). For ruffle, cut five strips of fabric 16cm/6¼″ by 90cm/36″ and one strip 16cm/6¼″ by 42cm/16½″. Sew strips together end-to-end to form a circle. Press seams and fold in half lengthwise, wrong sides together. Sew ruffle to needlepoint (see page 156). Cut and sew the backing (see page 156).

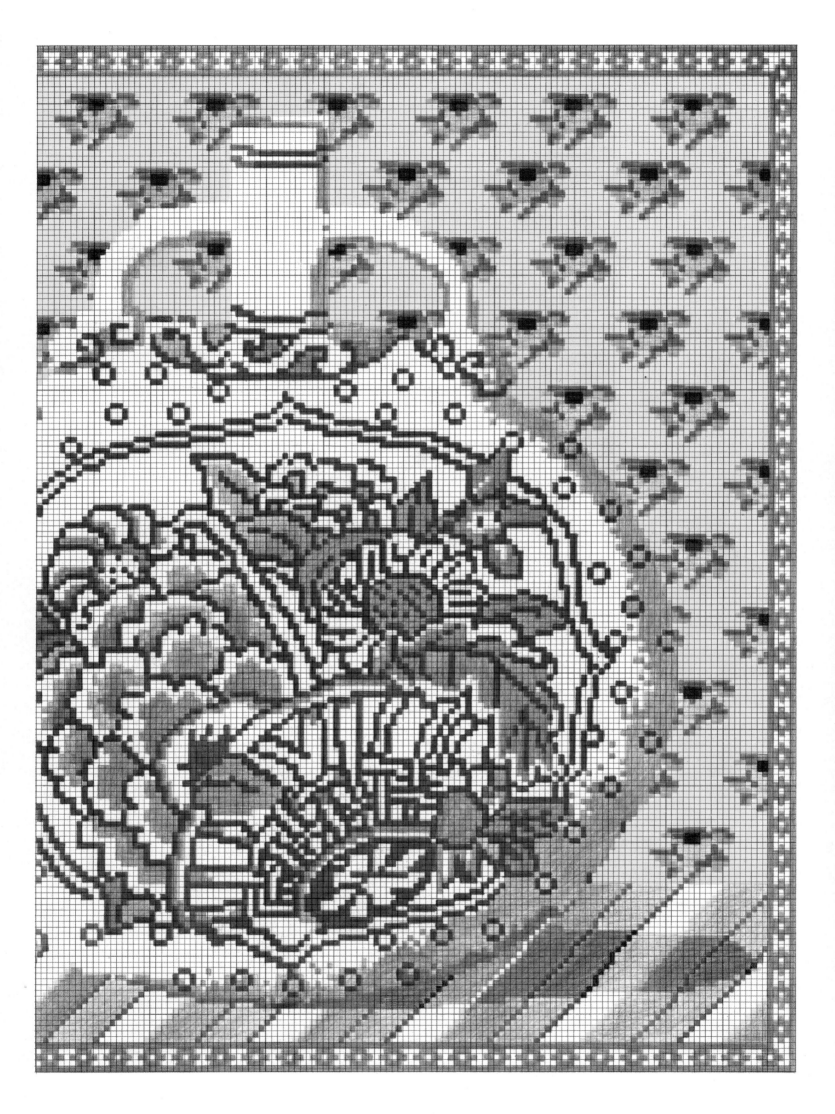

■ (Right) These
larger-than-life china
pots make a gorgeous
glow on my studio
wall.

■ (Opposite page)
Me, trying to give
some scale to this 2m/
6ft tapestry.

CHINA POT TAPESTRY

This tapestry grew out of my love for the two huge jars in the background. Their strong, colourful decoration shed a happy glow over my studio and begged to be recorded in some way. I did a rough painting in acrylic to start, using several other pots placed on an old 1940 curtain, with my flower bench tapestry (page 72) on the wall behind. I am particularly pleased with the glow of warm gold into orange, balanced with cool blues. You will notice that I have copied the designs on the pots fairly flatly, with only a hint of shadow to give a sense of dimension. I have often noticed how the Chinese and Indians paint in this flat manner and find it quite easy to achieve amazingly complex results.

Working on a large scale is not as daunting as it might appear. I sewed two strips of 5-mesh canvas together and drew out my design. I divided my painting into 5cm/2″ squares with taped-on cotton strings. Then I drew corresponding squares onto the canvas, which helped me quickly to draw the shapes up to scale. With the help of four students and some faithful friends, we stitched in long stitch with two strands of tapestry yarn and one crewel per needle. The whole piece took only three months to complete and measures 2m/6ft by 2.5m/8ft. It was suspended on a baton with pulleys, so it could be lowered to work on and pulled back up to observe at frequent intervals.

PLAID CUSHIONS

Plaids have a classic appeal that goes back to the earliest woven textiles. They can be bold or fine, monotone or filled with complex overlapping colours. Japanese woodcuts and Indian miniatures often show handsome robes of simple plaids. In Scotland they became an art form, and many of the richly coloured ancient tweeds survive in fashion to this day. The new versions are not as subtle in colouring as their predecessors, but with your needlepoint you can recapture the glory of the past.

Steve has placed these two plaids on a delightful wicker chair in a room of toy ships. The rag rug is a masterpiece of joyful freedom. The multicoloured ropes surrounding this running black cat would

(Right) I love the way these autumn leaves and the old cotton-print umbrella go with this beigey-grey plaid.

make any artist proud to put his or her name to it, and I am sure it was done by someone with no formal art training.

Plaids can make wonderful borders or backings (see page 30). Any colour scheme can be echoed in a plaid, so you should have fun using many differing combinations of colours. I particularly like the pastel-and-cream balls on the rug. These two cushions are very subdued browns and beiges and could work in a smart modern room.

MATERIALS FOR FINE PLAID CUSHION

Appleton tapestry wool in the following colours and approximate amounts (see page 152):

▨	821 (18.3m/20yd)	▨	182 (58m/63yd)
▨	602 (18.3m/20yd)	▨	763 (61m/67yd)
▨	961 (53m/58yd)	☐	992 (16m/17yd)
▨	963 (20m/22yd)	▨	203 (23m/25yd)
▨	967 (27m/29yd)	▣	993 (64m/70yd)
▨	184 (20m/22yd)		

10-mesh double-thread or interlocked canvas 50cm/20" square
80cm/1yd of 90cm/36" backing fabric and matching thread
1.7m/2yd of piping cord
30cm/12" zip fastener (optional)
Finished needlepoint measures approximately 40cm/16" square.

MATERIALS FOR BOLD PLAID CUSHION

Appleton tapestry wool in the following colours and approximate amounts (see page 152):

▨	961 (35m/39yd)	▨	974 (14m/15yd)

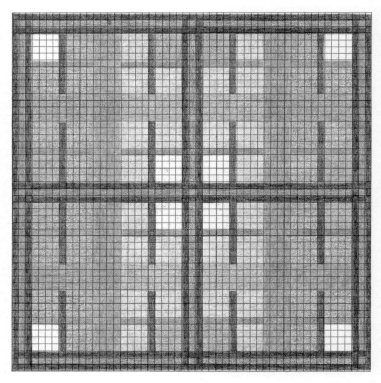

743 (18m/20yd)   976 (64m/70yd)
992 (22m/24yd)   184 (82m/90yd)
973 (37m/40yd)   993 (72m/78yd)

10-mesh double-thread or interlocked canvas 50cm/20″ square
80cm/1yd of 90cm/36″ backing fabric and matching thread
1.7m/2yd of piping cord

30cm/12″ zip fastener (optional)
Finished needlepoint measures approximately 40cm/16″ square.

WORKING PLAID CUSHIONS
Both finished plaid needlepoints are 161 stitches square. For each, mark the outline onto the canvas and make a template (see

(Below) This collection of ships and the rag rug would make good needlepoint. The classic neutral plaids seem to fit well anywhere.

■ (Below) You can see that the design on the carpet bag would make a handsome cushion, particularly with colours like this trunk.

■ (Opposite page) Detail of carpet bag.

page 155). Following the chart (see page 154), place the centre stitch of the chart at the centre of the canvas and work the embroidery in tent stitch using *one strand* of tapestry wool. After completing the chart, repeat the plaid pattern from the centre outwards until the needlepoint is 161 stitches square. Block the finished needlepoint (see page 155). Cut and sew the backing and piping (see page 156).

CARPET BAG

The playfulness of crude, geometric flowers in Oriental carpets has always delighted me. I wanted to do my own version of these carpets as a bag with borders. It is great fun to stitch. The more primitive it looks, the better. I have kept the colours dark and rich but you certainly could do this in many different combinations. Antique, sandy colours with dull, pastel tones would be gorgeous.

The strap is on the wide side, as both it and the bag are done on 7-mesh canvas with double yarn. You could do the strap on 10-mesh canvas, with single colours, which would make a thinner strap. The lining can be any fabric that strikes your fancy. A stripe in dark, dull colours or blue denim would be handsome. The strap pattern would make another good belt or hat band, in a finer mesh.

MATERIALS FOR CARPET BAG

Appleton tapestry wool in the following colours and approximate amounts (see page 152):

▨ 182 (111m/122yd)		▨ 221 (74m/81yd)	
▨ 952 (94m/103yd)		▨ 223 (82m/90yd)	
▨ 693 (91m/100yd)		▉ 927 (196m/215yd)	
▉ 503 (110m/120yd)		▉ 924 (89m/97yd)	
▨ 145 (96m/105yd)		▨ 563 (79m/86yd)	
▉ 126 (110m/120yd)		▉ 716 (196m/215yd)	

7-mesh double-thread or interlocked canvas 90cm/36" by 125cm/50"
1.1m/1¼yd of 90cm/36" lining fabric and matching thread
Finished back or front measures approximately 38cm/15" by 43cm/17¼", strap approximately 161cm/64½" by 9cm/3½" and bottom approximately 38cm/15" by 9cm/3½".

WORKING CARPET BAG

The bag is worked in four pieces: front, back, strap and bottom. The chart for the front or back is 105 stitches wide by 121 stitches high. The chart for the strap is 25 stitches wide by 250 stitches long, and is repeated until the strap is 452 stitches long. The chart for the bottom is 25 stitches wide by 105 stitches long. Mark outlines for the front, back, strap and bottom onto the canvas and make templates (see page 155). Following the chart (see page 154), work the embroidery for the first side in tent stitch using *two strands* of tapestry wool together. Work the second side in the same way. To read the strap chart, turn the book sideways so that page 133 is at the top. Following the chart, work the embroidery until line 1 is reached, then turn the chart and work backwards from line 2 to beginning of chart (452 stitches in length). This completes the strap. For the bottom of the bag, work the chart from line 3 to line 4. Block the finished needlepoints (see page 155). Cut pieces of lining the same sizes as front, back, strap and bottom, plus a 1.5cm/⅝" seam allowance. With right sides facing, sew bottom to back and front, then sew strap to back and front along sides. Trim canvas to 1cm/½" around needlepoint pieces. Fold the canvas edge back all around and join all the pieces, as for the lining but with the wrong sides facing, and working a half-cross-stitch seam with 927 (see page 155). Insert lining into bag. Turn under hems of lining and needlepoint along top edges of bag and along strap. Stitch lining to needlepoint with an invisible seam.

STRIPED KNITTING BAG

Another carpet design that often rivets me is diagonal stripes, so I borrowed that idea, added a border and worked it all in jolly, summery colours. My first attempt at the bag had a dark border that did not seem quite right, so I started again and used the curry-

▨ *(Above) This old carpet, that graced my studio floor, fed me the idea for the carpet bag.*

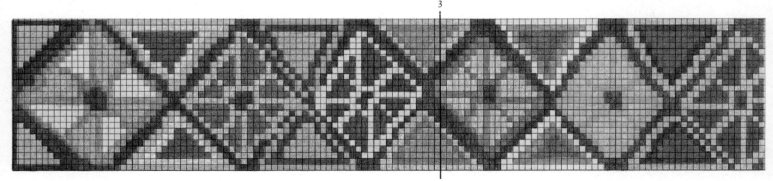

3

3

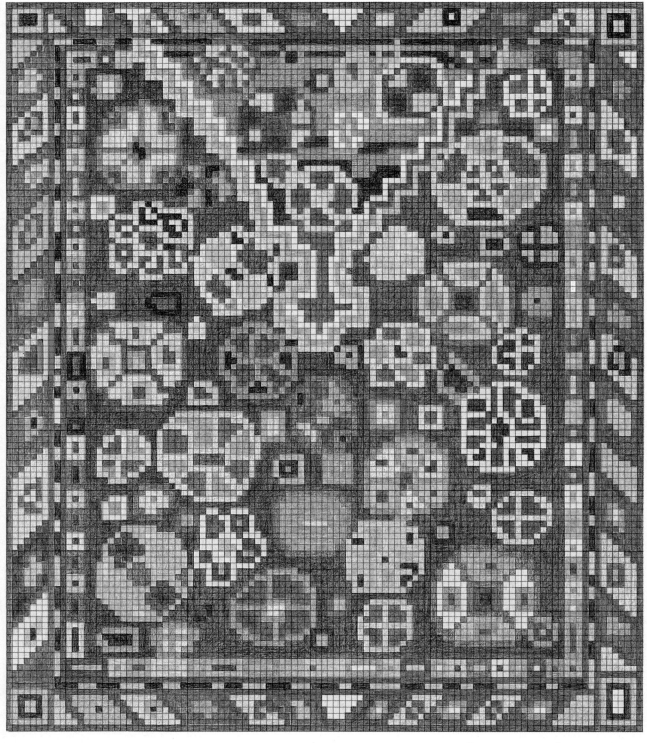

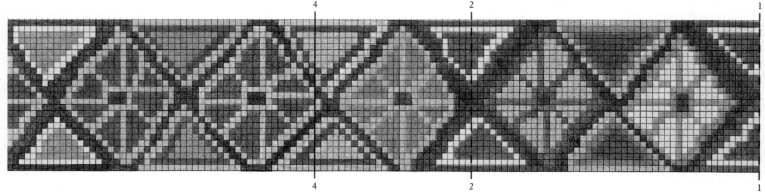

4   2   1

4   2   1

(Previous page)
The diagonal-striped
knitting bag looking
summery in a Sussex
garden.

(Below) Detail of
knitting bag.

yellow as a ground for the half-flowers on the border. Reds, whites and blues, if muted in tone, would make a striking bag in this pattern, or go for dark, rich colours like those of the carpet bag on page 131.

MATERIALS FOR STRIPED KNITTING BAG

Appleton tapestry wool in the following colours and approximate amounts (see page 152):

■	924 (236m/258yd)	▨	203 (177m/194yd)
▨	561 (89m/97yd)	▨	473 (133m/145yd)
▨	461 (74m/81yd)	■	865 (106m/116yd)
▨	463 (118m/129yd)	■	866 (24m/26yd)
▨	251 (118m/129yd)	☐	841 (112m/123yd)
▨	754 (124m/136yd)		

7-mesh double thread or interlocked canvas 74cm/29¾" by 110cm/43½"

45cm/½yd of 90cm/36" lining fabric and matching thread

Two handles (see page 157)

Finished needlepoint measures approximately 45cm/17¾" by 64cm/25¾" across bottom and 47cm/18¾" across top.

WORKING STRIPED KNITTING BAG

The chart is 125 stitches high by 180 stitches wide, across the bottom. Mark the outline onto the canvas for the first side and make a template (see page 155). To read the chart, turn the book sideways so that the centre of the book is at the top. Following the chart (see page 154), work the embroidery in tent stitch using *two strands* of tapestry wool together. Repeat for the second side. Block the finished needlepoints (see page 155). With the right sides facing, join the needlepoints along the sides and lower edges, leaving 20cm/7¾" open on top at each side. Trim seams and turn bag right side out. Slip handles over tops of front and back, and fold hem down along lower edge of checks at top (see page 157 for making handles). Stitch hem in place. Cut two pieces of lining the same size as the needlepoint front and back, plus a 1.5cm/⅝" seam allowance all around the edges. With the right sides facing, sew the lining together leaving the top open at each side, as for the needlepoint bag. Insert lining into bag. Turn under hem of lining and stitch to needlepoint with an invisible seam.

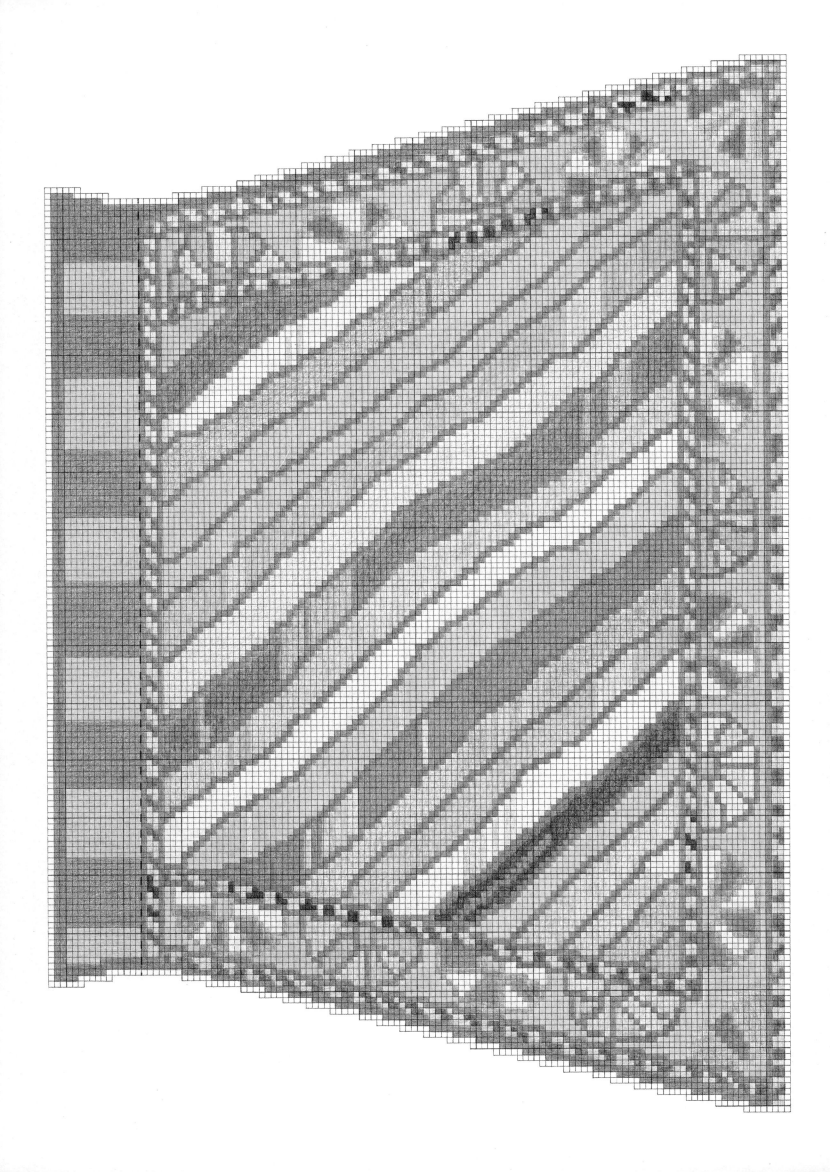

(Right) You can see how joins were made in this twelve-person effort. Each stitcher worked with his or her neighbours to line up the colours at the cross-over points, then went off to work quite separately with agreed background colours.

(Bottom right) The Cosmos tapestry as a country rug in an English country house.

(Opposite page) The entire Cosmos tapestry.

(Overleaf) These African masks and fabrics create a perfect ambience for the lichen frame.

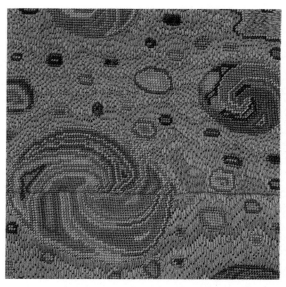

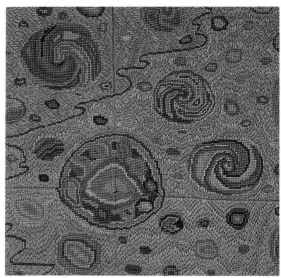

COSMOS TAPESTRY

This piece is a landmark in my needlepoint career. After stitching that first paperweight cushion, it occurred to me to do a big ambitious piece. I found a group of like-minded friends who were working in a house in the West Country of England. We wanted a communal activity to fill afternoons and evenings and we wanted to make something of beauty. For inspiration, I turned to early Celtic art – those myriad swirling circular shapes. I loved the way they dazzled the viewer with many intricate patterns and changes of scale. It was not at all difficult to adopt the same playful frame of mind and come up with several variations on the divisions of a circle.

I drew out two large circles and filled each one with many smaller ones. Some of these I divided into swirling lines to each centre; others I divided into crosses. Then I dumped about seventy-five colours on the floor and had each stitcher select what he or she fancied. Most of the stitchers had never done anything artistic before, let alone needlepoint. Each stitcher then went off with one-twelfth of the tapestry and completed his or her square. We came together only when we needed to match a crossing-over circle or background bit with its neighbour.

The cohesion of the finished piece astounded us all. It was achieved partly by weeding out any hard, bright colours from the first choice, keeping all the colours quite soft and natural in tone. Then, putting the seventy-five colours on the neutral, grey grounds helped. I had stipulated that the inner circle ground should have four soft shades of grey in sequence and that the outer area should have a more contrasting series of greys, creating a bolder pattern. This left enough creative choices to the stitchers to keep them highly motivated. They could make the background sequences go as they liked, creating amazing patterns, plus choosing the small circle colours.

We sewed it together with strands unravelled from the linen canvas. It was a joy to work on and I thoroughly recommend it to any group as a project.

LICHEN FRAME

Lichen on stone was one of my strongest British impressions when I got here in 1965. The astounding variety and subtle beauty of their shapes and soft colours is a whole miniature world to me. One of the things I first collected that feeds me constantly with inspiration is a piece of roof slate, covered in little lichens. I love the pale, delineated outline around each form. The lichen is quite easy and effective to imitate and makes a handsome picture frame. You could extend it to any size, and do it in colours that suit your furnishings. This theme would make a good cushion as a square. Think of it in soft peaches and creamy yellows, on a pale blue to look like a painted sky.

MATERIALS FOR LICHEN FRAME

Appleton crewel wool in the following colours and approximate amounts (see page 152):

971 (55m/60yd)	204 (27m/30yd)
931 (27m/30yd)	124 (37m/40yd)
332 (27m/30yd)	914 (2m/2yd)
334 (27m/30yd)	331 (62m/68yd)
981 (5.5m/6yd)	964 (17m/19yd)
952 (5.5m/6yd)	983 (15m/16yd)
967 (5.5m/6yd)	

10-mesh double-thread linen canvas 36cm/ 14¼" by 42cm/16¾"
Cardboard for frame
5cm/2" masking tape
Finished needlepoint measures approximately 26cm/10¼" by 32cm/12¾".

WORKING LICHEN FRAME

This needlepoint is for the more adventurous embroiderer who wants to try out toning effects (see page 154). Only the lichen outlines, the two rows of stitches at the outer edge of the frame, and the single row of stitches at the inner edge of the frame are given square for square (i.e. stitch for stitch) on the chart. The rest of the chart is coloured in to show the toning effect achieved by mixing the yarns, and cannot be followed square for square. Follow the guidelines below for mixing the colours.

The chart is 103 stitches wide by 128 stitches high. Mark the outline onto the canvas and make a template (see page 155). Following the chart (see page 154) and mixing the yarns, work the embroidery in tent stitch using *two strands* of crewel wool together. Begin by working the single row of stitches around the inner edge and the two rows of stitches around the outer edge, using one strand of 964 and one strand of 983 together. Work the lichen outlines using two strands of 331 together for most of the outlines, and one strand each of 331 and 971 together to soften the outlines in a few places. The base colour for the lichen (areas inside the outlined, rounded shapes) is 971. Fill in some of the lichen using two strands of 971 together. Then continue shading by using one strand of 971 (or one strand of 931 in a few areas), with one strand of one of the following colours: 931, 332, 334, 981, 952, or 967. The base colours for the background (areas outside the rounded shapes) are 204 and 124. Begin the background by using two strands of 204 together to shade in along the outer edge of the frame, blending gradually into using two strands of 124 together. Then continue shading by using one strand of 124 with one strand of one of the following colours: 967, 964, 332, 334, 971, 931, or 914. Block the finished needlepoint (see page 155). Make the frame and attach the canvas to the frame (see page 157).

SPECTACLES CASES AND YELLOW RUG

Here is a perfect example of the sheer joy and inventiveness of geometrics. The spectacles cases are quick and easy to do,

(Left) The source for the lichen frame rests against the canvas set in a friend's West Country garden. This stone urn would make a gorgeous needlepoint.

■ *(Below right) The spectacles case has a panel of blue-and-pink checks which is turned under for the hem. You could dispense with these six rows and line with a bright print.*

■ *(Opposite page) The spectacles cases rest on my yellow geometric table carpet. It was interesting to see these African beaded gourds next to the needlepoint that has such a beaded look.*

playing with squares, circles and diamonds. With all this colour they have a beaded look, particularly with their little, contrasting borders. You could make quite a jolly cushion or purse by repeating the pink-and-green spectacles case four times, omitting the chequerboard top.

The yellow table rug was my travelling project on a tour of New Zealand and Japan in 1986. I stitched away on buses, planes, trains and in hotel rooms. The beauty of it was not having to refer to any source material. I just improvised my colours and shapes, crowding the yellow space with as many variations of circles, squares and triangles as I could cram in. You will notice that I used only single rows of stitches for each contrasting colour in the motifs. I bought yarn as I went along. If I could not find enough bright colours in tapestry yarn, I would use knitting and darning yarns. The background is composed of at least twenty-

five yellows and golds. For this bright palette I found that the only thing that positively did not work were dull colours or very deep tones. When I put in some purple and dark maroon it was like punching holes in the design – the dark areas leapt out of the composition of light, bright colour. So I unpicked these areas.

MATERIALS FOR CIRCLES SPECTACLES CASE

Appleton tapestry wool in the following colours and approximate amounts (see page 152):

▨	552 (5.5m/6yd)	■	145 (3.7m/4yd)
■	464 (5.5m/6yd)	▨	751 (6.4m/7yd)
▨	431 (18m/20yd)	□	841 (4.6m/5yd)
■	625 (2.8m/3yd)	▨	482 (6.4m/7yd)
▨	943 (20m/22yd)	□	991b (3.7m/4yd)
▨	461 (2.8m/3yd)		

10-mesh double-thread or interlocked canvas 26cm/10½" by 28cm/11¼"
Small amount of lining fabric and matching thread
Finished needlepoint measures approximately 16cm/6½" by 18cm/7¼" and finished case measures approximately 8cm/3¼" by 17cm/6¾".

WORKING CIRCLES SPECTACLES CASE

The chart is 64 stitches wide by 73 stitches high. Mark the outline onto the canvas and make a template (see page 155). Following the chart (see page 154), work the embroid-

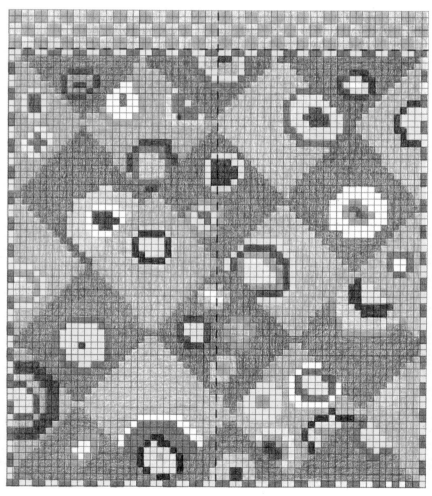

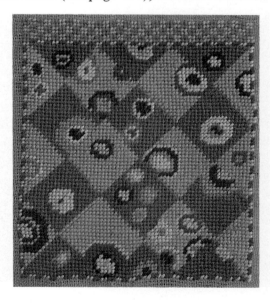

144

■ *(Below)*
Watercolour
medallion rug from
my sketch book.

■ *(Far right) The*
medallion cushions
look right at home in
this mélange of
Eastern textiles, my
favourite being the
fine silk needlepoint
coat hanging on the
left.

ery in tent stitch using *one strand* of tapestry wool. Block the finished needlepoint (see page 155). Trim canvas to 1cm/½″ around needlepoint. Fold canvas edge back all around. Fold hem down at top, along lower edge of checks. Cut lining the same size as the needlepoint, plus 1.5cm/⅝″ seam allowance. Fold back seam allowance all around lining and pin to needlepoint. Stitch lining to needlepoint. Fold needlepoint in half lengthwise so that wrong sides are together. Join seam of spectacles case with half cross stitch (see page 155) using 943.

MEDALLION CUSHIONS

I was particularly struck by the bold medallion in the centre of this terracotta rug. The idea of two huge cushions to go with it seemed a good plan. Working from the carpet, matching colours and forms, was an excellent way to observe how freely drawn most carpet design is. It seems to grow organically, only roughly bowing to symmetry. Yet the whole thing adds up to a perfect balance. This gave me the courage to draw quickly and freely onto my canvas and not to be fussy about making each part of the design exactly match its counterpart. The discrepancies, indeed, give the stitching its authentic human feeling. Due to the

146

■ *(Right) The carpet source for the medallion cushion. You can see from the in-progress shot how crudely the mirror image is worked out, so that it does not give mechanical stiffness to the repeat. The outlines should go in first to give crisp shapes.*

colour as possible, as most modern carpets are too simplistic in colouring.

MATERIALS FOR MEDALLION CUSHION

Appleton tapestry wool in the following colours and approximate amounts (see page 152):

■ 124 (163m/181yd)	■ 994 (273m/303yd)
■ 222 (76m/84yd)	■ 151 (15m/16yd)
■ 224 (93m/103yd)	■ 154 (24m/26yd)
■ 241 (209m/232yd)	■ 181 (342m/380yd)
■ 693 (59m/65yd)	■ 972 (55m/61yd)
■ 504 (24m/26yd)	■ 929 (324m/355yd)

7-mesh double-thread or interlocked canvas 94cm/37¾" square
90cm/1yd of 90cm/36" backing fabric and matching thread
3.5m/4yd piping cord
66cm/26" zip fastener (optional)
Finished needlepoint measures approximately 84cm/33¾" square.

WORKING MEDALLION CUSHION

The finished medallion needlepoint is 236 stitches wide by 236 stitches high. (The chart is for one quarter of the cushion and is 118 stitches wide by 118 stitches high.) Mark the outline for one quarter of the cushion onto the canvas and make a template (see page 155). Following the chart (see page 154), work the embroidery in tent stitch in one corner of the design using *two strands* of tapestry wool together.

For the other sections of the medallion needlepoint, trace the first quarter onto tracing paper. Outline the traced shapes onto the three other sections, reversing the shapes where appropriate. When tracing the shapes onto the needlepoint canvas, vary each section slightly to avoid deadly symmetry.

Fill in the other sections of the medallion, using the first section as a guide for colours. You will see that there are variation tones for red and pink sections. Feel free to add tones to navy and cream areas for an authentic carpet feeling. Block the finished needlepoint (see page 155). Cut and sew the backing and piping (see page 156). If desired, edge with cord instead of piping, giving careful thought to your choice of colour.

vegetable dyes and handspun yarns, the actual carpet has many shades in each colour. I used combinations of several pinks to achieve that feeling.

We have graphed out one quarter of the medallion design here, which you could draw onto your canvas. You could then quite freely mirror-image it, and get your own differences into each quarter. Since flea markets, carpet shops and museums are overflowing with interesting old carpets, you should be able to gather many ideas for your own versions of carpet patterns. Books and postcards of carpets are easy to study at your leisure and you can adapt the colours to suit your rooms. Always add as much

■ *(From top left to right) Carpet Garden, Night Tree, Harvest Bowl, Leafy, Baroda Stripe, Sea Bird, Paisley, Peony Jar.*

EHRMAN KITS

I started designing for Hugh Ehrman in the late Seventies. His growing expertise in commissioning and marketing these kits has made them available to a large audience. His catalogue includes the work of other textile designers as well as a selection of my knitting kits.

Here are ten of my favourite needlepoint designs for cushions. They are all available as kits from Ehrman (see page 158). Carpet Garden, Night Tree and Baroda Stripe were directly inspired by Oriental carpets. Carpet Garden comes with a black or red ground. Any two of these sewn together would make a handsome bag.

Harvest Bowl was a border detail on an old tapestry, where I tried to achieve the same weathered colours as the antique textile. The colours look wonderful with stone and wood tones.

Leafy is designed to fit various chair seats. The background can be expanded for larger chairs or just a portion of the central leaves can be used for small chairs or cushions. This simple all-over needlepoint design could be done in more vivid autumn colours for a change of mood.

The Sea Bird cushion needlepoint occurred to me when studying ornate Chinese decorated-beam ceilings. These ceilings are usually vivid reds, blues and greens, but I favoured these soft pastels with black and red accents.

Paisley is taken from Kashmiri shawls which originated in Northern India and are a wonderful source of design for needlepoint. The paisley flower forms make gorgeous carpets, as you can see in most antique carpet shops or textile museums.

Peony Jar is a romantic portrait of my favourite Chinese jar (also seen in China pot tapestry on page 127). You will see that the original jar had deep royal blue, lemon yellow and raspberry pink – do feel free to jazz up any subdued colouring, if you fancy more punch!

Star Tile and Fresco Star are from Islamic tile themes. These again would make good bags sewn together and lined like the carpet bag on page 131. Their geometric patterns and subdued colours make them blend into most settings.

Several of my other needlepoints are also available as kits from Ehrman and are listed on page 158).

■ (Left) Star Tile.

■ (Below) Fresco Star.

NEEDLEPOINT TECHNIQUES

The emotional impact of colour and pattern is my top priority. I am bothered about technique only enough to produce a lasting article. If the technicalities start to get in my way, I bend the rules to facilitate the creative flow of improvisation. So, do not take the techniques that follow as steadfast rules, but more as helpful and flexible guidelines for working the needlepoints that are charted in this book. If you are a beginner, you will pick up needlepoint methods by just getting on with it and learning by your mistakes. Reading what follows may help you avoid some of the more obvious initial pitfalls.

NEEDLEPOINT CANVAS
Unlike other forms of embroidery which are worked on ordinary fabric, needlepoint is worked on an evenweave canvas. The canvas comes in various gauges or mesh sizes, ranging from the finest with 32 holes or threads per 2.5cm/1″ to the largest with 3 holes per 2.5cm/1″. The finer gauges are used for the tiny, detailed stitches of petit-point and the bigger gauges for needlepoint rugs. I generally prefer using a medium mesh size of 10 holes to the 2.5cm/1″, or a slightly larger 7-mesh canvas. These two mesh sizes give me a stitch size that is small enough to create the detail I want but big enough for my stitching to proceed rapidly.

Apart from coming in different gauges, the canvas also comes in three different types – mono (or single-thread) canvas, interlocked canvas and double-thread (or Penelope) canvas. It is largely a case of personal taste which type of canvas you prefer to work with. If you are doing petit-point, mono canvas is a must because it is the only type that comes in the finer mesh sizes from 32- to 16-mesh. I like double-thread or interlocked canvas for everything but petit-point, because you can work all types of stitches on it, including half cross stitch. With double-thread canvas, the threads can be split apart in areas so that it converts to mono canvas. In this way fine stitches for details can be combined on the same canvas with larger stitches for backgrounds, for instance. Double-thread canvas is usually softer, too, because it has not been stiffened as much and the individual threads are finer than the individual threads of a mono canvas of the same gauge. Interlocked canvas is stiffer, but because the threads are locked together it does not fray as easily or distort during stitching as much as the other types.

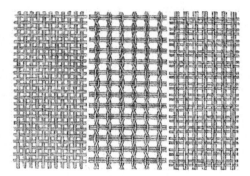

BUYING CANVAS
When buying canvas for the needlepoints in this book, for best results buy the type of canvas that is suggested. But do not worry about getting the *exact* mesh size, if it is not available to you. One stitch per inch, more or less, will not make much difference to the size of the finished needlepoint. You may even want to alter the size of the needlepoint – say for a larger or smaller cushion. The charts can be worked on any gauge of canvas. Just be sure to buy enough canvas to allow for 5cm/2″ extra all around the design. Also remember that a much larger gauge will require more yarn and the addition of more strands of yarn to cover the canvas threads.

YARNS
Several types of yarns are suitable for needlepoint. I like using yarns that come in a vast range of delicious colours. When you are buying yarns for the needlepoints in this book you will be able to duplicate my design exactly, if you use the same brand and the same colour numbers. If you want to substitute yarns of another brand, use the photos as a guide for the colours. The chart colours do not always exactly match the actual yarn colours, as the artist has often had to exaggerate colour differences to make the chart readable.

But do not think you have to stick to my colours. Be brave and make your own choices, or even add more colours! The only tip to keep in mind is that you will need a yarn that is thick enough to cover the canvas threads. The standard wool needlepoint yarns come in three thicknesses – crewel, tapestry and Persian. Crewel wool is quite fine and at least three crewel strands together are needed for a 10-mesh canvas. It is perfect for mixing your own tones and colours (see page 154). Tapestry wool is thicker and a single strand will cover a 10-mesh canvas. Two strands of tapestry wool are needed for a 7-mesh canvas. Persian wool is made up of three strands of yarn that can be easily separated. Spun slightly more tightly than tapestry wool, although of a similar thickness, Persian wool gives a lovely texture to fringes on needlepoint rugs.

I am often accused of not covering my canvas properly with wool. Sometimes I like the threadbare look of soft colours on linen canvas (white canvas showing through is always nasty-looking to my eye). If you find your stitch tension is causing the canvas to show unintentionally in places, just add a strand of crewel to your yarn to bulk out each stitch. I sometimes wait till my canvas is stretched to see what is ironed out in that process, and then carefully add stitches to cover the worst gaps.

BUYING YARNS
When purchasing yarns for my needlepoint designs, remember that the amounts given are only approximate. The amounts are estimated for basketweave or continental tent stitch. The half-cross technique takes about one-third less yarn. The amounts needed may vary from one embroiderer to the next according to how loosely or tightly you stitch. It is a good idea to buy only part of the yarn required to begin with, and then estimate how much more is needed after part of the canvas has been worked. Keep a record of the dye lot for your background colour, if you want to be sure to match it perfectly. It is really not necessary to match precisely other colours which are sprinkled throughout the needlepoint, because varying dye lots just add to the beauty of the work.

NEEDLEPOINT STITCHES
There are many types of stitches which have been developed for needlepoint. Generally I work in tent stitch or random long stitch, because they are quick and easy and give the type of texture I like for my designs. You may want to stretch your canvas on an embroidery frame, before stitching onto the canvas. Frames can be found at most local sewing shops. Personally I like working needlepoint handheld, because I find it easier to manipulate and perfect for carrying with me wherever I go. But it is important for each embroiderer to do what is most comfortable. Working with a frame leaves two hands free to pass the needle back and forth from front to back, and also keeps the embroidery from being distorted if you tend to stitch too tightly. Try it both ways!

CONTINENTAL TENT STITCH
The three most popular techniques for forming the short, straight, slanted stitches of tent stitch are called continental, basketweave and half cross. They all look the same from the front, and I use them alternately as the fancy takes me, even all on the same canvas! (For pale, solid backgrounds, however, it is best to stick to one type of stitch to avoid creating ridges on the right side of the work.)

Continental tent stitch forms long, slanted stitches on the reverse and can be worked on any type of needlepoint canvas. Before beginning, choose a blunt-ended tapestry needle, large enough to hold the yarn without damaging it, but not so large that it has to be forced through the canvas.

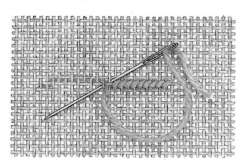

1. When beginning, leave a 2.5cm/1" long loose end at the back, and work the first few stitches from right to left over it, as shown here.

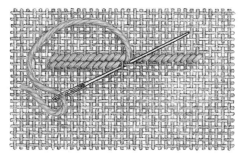

2. Work the following row of stitches below the last row. Continue working alternately from right to left, then from left to right.

BASKETWEAVE TENT STITCH
This technique may look a little more difficult, but it becomes second nature once you get the hang of it. It can be worked on any type of canvas and is good for covering large backgrounds, as it tends to keep the canvas from biasing. Be sure not to use too long a piece of yarn – 30cm/15" is plenty. If your yarn is too long it will twist and tangle and slow you down.

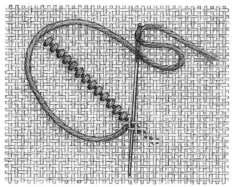

1. Work over the loose end at the back, when beginning (see continental tent stitch). The first row is worked downwards diagonally from left to right, forming vertical stitches at the back.

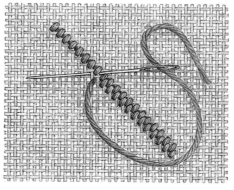

2. The following row is worked upwards

from right to left, slotting in between the stitches of the previous row. Horizontal stitches are formed at the back on this row. Continue repeating the downward and upward rows alternately.

HALF CROSS STITCH
The half cross-stitch technique uses less yarn than the other two tent-stitch techniques. This is because the stitches at the back of the work are short, vertical stitches that do not cover the back of the canvas. When an entire design is worked in half cross stitch the resulting needlepoint is not as thick as a needlepoint worked in basketweave or continental tent stitch. Half cross stitch cannot be worked on mono canvas. It requires a double-thread or interlocked canvas.

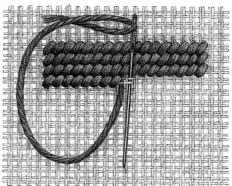

Work over the loose end at the back, when beginning (see continental tent stitch). Work in rows alternately from left to right and right to left, making short vertical stitches at the back as shown here. When ending a length of yarn, pass it through a few stitches at the back or merely catch it into the next row.

RANDOM LONG STITCH
This stitch is fabulous for filling in large areas of background fast! Or even for working entire, large needlepoint wall hangings (see pages 72–73, 82, 112–113, 127, and 139).

Make sure you use a double-thread canvas and a thick enough strand of yarn to cover the canvas threads. For some mesh sizes a single strand of tapestry wool is almost thick enough, but not quite, and two strands of tapestry wool together is just too bulky. In such a case try adding a single strand of crewel yarn or, if necessary, two strands of crewel yarn.

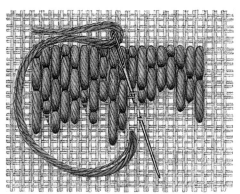

The random long stitch should be worked in varying lengths along each row. Work one row from right to left, then the following row from left to right, and so on alternately.

SHADING, TONING AND CREATING COLOURS

Once you have learnt random long stitch or traditional tent stitch you can let your fingers do the stitching and concentrate on lovely colours and beautiful designs. Needlepoint yarns come in wide ranges of colours, but you can also mix your own. I always keep a selection of crewel wool yarns for this purpose. If I run out of a particular colour or if the colour I want just does not exist, I mix my own. All that is needed are two or three different colours of crewel yarn close to the shade required. These are all threaded together into the needle and usually do the trick. Mixing crewel strands is especially handy for subtle shading, like that on my Kabuki face cushion.

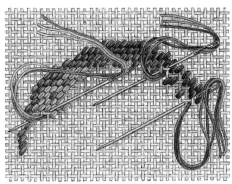

For subtle shading effects take three shades of crewel in the chosen colour – dark, medium and light. Work the shading by using two strands of the darkest shade with one strand of the medium shade, for the darkest areas. Then gradually lighten the colour by using two strands of the medium

shade with only one strand of the darkest shade, and so on. Overlap the rows by sprinkling a few stitches of the adjacent shade into the next shade. This keeps distinct lines from forming. The difference in colours is exaggerated here, so you can see where one shade ends and the next begins, but in reality the shades blend together imperceptibly. The same could be done for changing gradually, not from darker to lighter, but from one colour to another, as in the pink blush on a golden mango.

NEEDLEPOINT DESIGNS

Every needlepoint enthusiast has the ability to create original designs. All it takes is canvas, yarn in an assortment of exciting colours and the courage to let your imagination go. Instructions for many of my own designs are given in the book for you to work from, and hopefully they will inspire you to begin your own creations. Here are some tips to consider before beginning a needlepoint, whether it is an original design or one you are working from a chart.

TRANSFERRING AN ORIGINAL DESIGN

When creating your own designs, you must first decide the size of the finished needlepoint. Draw these parameters onto a piece of paper and fill in your design. I generally only draw out the outlines of my shapes to scale and take the final details from my source material or from other sketches and watercolours. Choose the type and gauge of canvas you want to use (see page 152) and make sure you have a piece big enough to allow for 5cm/2″ extra canvas around the edge. For tracing the design you will need a green, red or blue waterproof pen. Avoid black, because it is difficult to see when stitching.

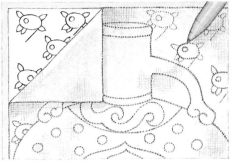

To trace the design, place the canvas over

your paper drawing and transfer the needlepoint parameter onto the canvas with a waterproof pen. Then trace the outlines of the pattern shapes onto the canvas. When the tracing is complete, make sure the ink is dry before beginning your needlepoint.

WORKING FROM CHARTS

The instructions for my needlepoints are all in chart form. The colours on the charts are not all exact reproductions of the original colours, because they often have to be slightly exaggerated to be distinguishable on the chart from the next colour. But the colour key provides the specific colour numbers. Remember there is no need to follow the chart, square for square. You can always work one area following the chart, then continue on your own, or you can work the outlines of the shapes from the chart, and fill in, using the chart merely as a general guide. And do not be afraid to add colours!

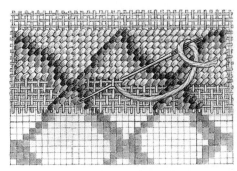

1. Each square on a tent-stitch needlepoint chart represents one tent stitch in the given colour. The equivalent of one square is a canvas mesh intersection and not a hole (see above).

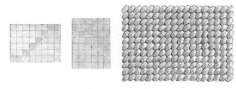

2. When reading charts, make sure that the top of the chart corresponds to the top of your needlepoint. For most of the charts in this book the top of the chart is at the top of the page. But read the instructions carefully before beginning, in case the chart needs to be turned sideways to be read correctly. If the chart is worked from the wrong direction, the shapes will be

altered. For instance, narrow lines slanting up from left to right will not be joined together (see above).

PREPARING THE CANVAS AND MAKING A TEMPLATE

If your canvas is white and you are using very dark colours in your needlepoint, it is a good idea to tint the canvas before beginning your needlepoint. Even the slightest gap in the yarn will allow the white to glare through, if it contrasts too sharply with the yarns. Take a watered-down solution of acrylic paint and brush it over the canvas. The most important part of preparing your canvas is making a paper template from the canvas outline. The finished needlepoint measurements given in the instructions are only approximate, and the final blocking should be done following the original size of the canvas outline.

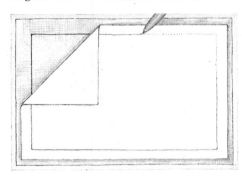

1. When working from a chart, mark the outline of the needlepoint with a waterproof pen onto the canvas. Count the canvas threads to determine the size – one intersection of canvas for each chart square, across both the length and width of the design. Allow at least 5cm/2" extra outside the outline. For curved shapes, mark lines across at the widest points. Trace the final outline onto a piece of paper and set this template aside for blocking.

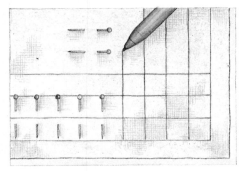

2. You may find it easier, when working

from a chart, to mark a grid onto the canvas, dividing it into tens just like the charted design. Before beginning the needlepoint, the edges of the canvas can be turned under and hemmed or tape can be folded over the edges to prevent fraying. Personally, I have never found it necessary to secure the canvas edges for working in the hand, as long as there is at least 5cm/2" extra canvas all around the needlepoint.

BLOCKING AND SIZING

While working your needlepoint, do not worry if it seems to become slightly distorted as the stitching progresses. The wool yarns are very amenable to being flattened and straightened into shape after the needlepoint has been completed. Your guide for blocking is the template of the original size of the unworked canvas outline.

After the needlepoint has been blocked, the shape can be sized or fixed on the back with wallpaper paste. The paste will give the needlepoint more body and resilience. It also usually contains a fungicide which helps preserve the yarns. I prefer the type of paste which dries clear instead of a milky opaque colour. Always check the contents of the paste to make sure it will not damage the needlepoint fibres, or ask your local needlepoint shop which type of paste they recommend. If a frame has been used, paste may not be needed.

When nailing the needlepoint in place for blocking you need not do it in the order I suggest. Some people nail one entire side before going on to the next. But be sure to use at least one tack per 2.5cm/1".

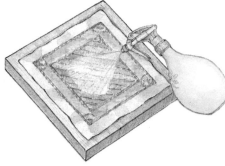

1. To block the finished needlepoint, place it face down and dampen it thoroughly by spraying it with water, or using a damp cloth or sponge.

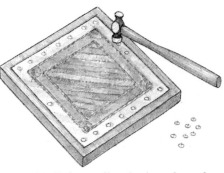

2. Nail the needlepoint into shape face down on a sheet of plywood, using your paper template as a guide. Begin with a nail at the centre of each side, then work outwards to the corners (see above). Allow the needlepoint to dry completely before removing, even if it takes several days.

3. Use a wallpaper paste to fix the shape, if desired. Mix the wallpaper paste to a fairly thick consistency. With the needlepoint still nailed in place, brush a light film of paste into the back. Remove only when completely dry.

HALF CROSS-STITCH SEAMS

This type of decorative seam is the best method for joining two pieces of needlepoint along a straight fold line. When a half cross-stitch seam appears in a needlepoint instruction, the colour of yarn to be used will be specified.

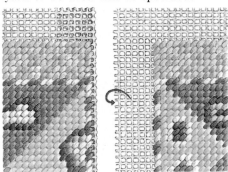

1. Trim the canvas edge to about 1.5cm/

155

¹/2" and turn back the canvas along the seam line. The fold should run across the next line of canvas thread, and not across the canvas holes. Place the needlepoints so that the right sides are facing you, and the edges are lined up row by row.

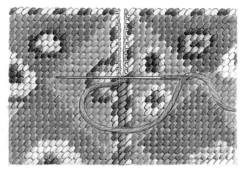

2. Using a blunt-ended tapestry needle, fasten the needlepoint yarn to the back of the canvas and bring it through to the front, through the first hole of the right-hand piece. Then pass the needle through the second hole of the adjacent piece, and back through the next hole on the right-hand piece. Continue in the same way up the seam, forming half cross stitches. When the seam has been completed, fasten off the yarn at the back of the work.

WASHING NEEDLEPOINT

Needlepoint does not need to be washed very often, if it has been worked with wool yarns. If it does become dirty over the years, you can wash it or have it dry cleaned. Be sure to check whether the yarns you have used for embroidering have any special washing or dry-cleaning instructions, before taking the plunge. Also, if in doubt, test your backing fabric to make sure it is colourfast. For washing, use warm water and a mild soap. It is best to use the bathtub, so that the needlepoint can be placed flat in the soapy water without being folded or wrinkled. Place the needlepoint face down in soapy water and press up and down on the back with a sponge, without rubbing. Change the water frequently when rinsing and do not wring the needlepoint. When the rinsing is complete let the last rinse water drain away and use a clean, dry sponge to soak up the remaining excess water. Then reblock the piece as above.

BACKING A CUSHION

Most of the needlepoint charts I have included in the book are for cushions. Backing a cushion is a fairly simple process and the drawings shown here should be a helpful visual guide. Only the most elementary sewing skills are needed. Hand and machine stitching are equally suitable. Put careful consideration into the colours you choose for the backing, because you want them to enhance rather than detract from your needlepoint. I find that fine wools and medium-weight cottons make the best backings. Including a zipper is an option that comes in handy when washing time rolls around.

Cut the lining, using the blocked needlepoint as a guide for size, and adding a 1.5cm/⅝" seam allowance. If inserting a zip fastener, cut two pieces, adding the seam allowance on both sides of the zipper as well.

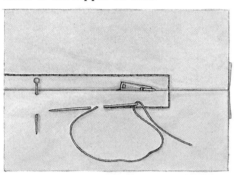

1. If inserting a zip fastener, begin by joining each end of the centre seam. Leave enough seam open at the middle for the length of the zipper. Pin the zip fastener in place and stitch, using backstitch or a sewing machine with a zipper foot.

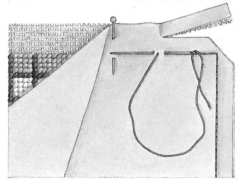

2. Pin the backing to the needlepoint with the right sides together. Using backstitch or a sewing machine, stitch close to the needlepoint all around the edge. Trim the seam edge and clip diagonally across the corners. Turn right side out. If no zip

fastener is being inserted, leave a gap just big enough to turn the work right side out, and complete with an invisible seam. Work shaped cushions in exactly the same way but make slits along the shaped edges of the finished seams.

PIPING

Piping is an attractive finish for the edge of a cushion. Again be sure to get the colour right, matching the needlepoint background colour if in doubt. Printed fabrics and even plaids make lovely piping and there is no reason why you cannot use a piping fabric which is different from your backing. Piping is made by covering piping cord with a strip of fabric cut on the bias. The biased fabric allows the cord to bend at the corners without buckling.

1. Cut biased fabric strips about 5cm/2" to 8cm/3" wide, depending on the thickness of your cord. Join the strips where necessary by working a seam with the grain of the fabric. Press the seams. Fold the fabric over the cord and, using a matching thread, baste close to the cord.

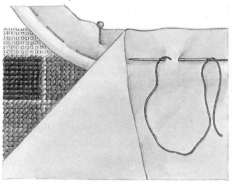

2. Pin the cord to the right side of the needlepoint so that the seam allowance runs along the bare canvas. Pin the lining in place over the piping and stitch in place with backstitch or a sewing machine. Trim seams and clip corners, finishing as for plain backing above.

RUFFLES

With the right fabric a ruffle can be a very effective decorative edging for a needlepoint (see pages 64 and 122). Cut the strips for the ruffles, so that they are twice the width of the desired finished ruffle, plus an extra 1.5cm/⅝" all around for the seam allowance. Sew the strips together end-to-end in a circle and press the seams. Fold the final strip in half lengthwise and press. The fabric is then ready to sew to the needlepoint.

Divide the ruffle into quarters and pin to the front of the needlepoint at each corner. Fold the pleats and pin in place along each edge, easing in extra fabric at each corner. Place the lining on top of the ruffle and stitch in place as for piping step 2.

MITRED FRAME

The Kabuki face cushion (pages 90–91) is a good example of how a fabric frame can be an integral part of your needlepoint design. In this case two colours – red and purple – were needed to achieve the desired effect. Patterned fabrics can sometimes be used for a more complex effect.

To begin the frame, cut fabric pieces on the straight grain of the fabric the length of each side, plus a 1.5cm/⅝" seam allowance. When working a double-colour frame, as for the Kabuki face cushion, start by sewing the two colours together lengthwise and pressing the seams. Repeat this process for each of the four sides.

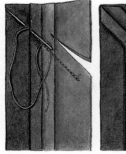

1. Join the first two strips diagonally at

the corners with backstitch or a sewing machine, leaving the seam allowance open at the inside edge (left). Trim the seam and press open (right). Repeat for the other three corners.

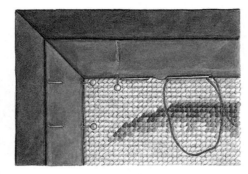

2. Fold the inside edge of the fabric under and pin the fabric to the edge of the needlepoint over the raw canvas. Using a matching thread, join with an invisible seam as shown.

MAKING HANDLES

If you cannot find ready-made handles for the knitting bag on page 136, you can make your own. All you need is a thin piece of plywood approximately 8mm/¼" thick, and a small jigsaw. Make a paper template of the handle shape. The opening for the bag should be wide enough for the top of the bag to fit through without being gathered up. It is best to finish and block the needlepoint before determining the shape of the handle, to ensure that it will fit properly.

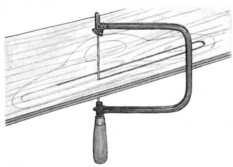

Trace the handle shape onto the piece of wood and cut out with the jigsaw. Do the same for the second handle. (Both handles can be cut at the same time by placing two pieces of wood together as shown above.) Smooth the edges carefully with sandpaper. If desired, coat the finished handles with a matt varnish, or paint and decorate with a pattern.

PICTURE FRAME

Here is a guide for making the picture frame for the lichen needlepoint on pages 140 and 141. You will need a large piece of stiff cardboard and a strong masking tape. Before beginning, block the finished needlepoint and let it dry. Then make a paper template of the finished needlepoint. Using this template, trace the shape onto a piece of cardboard. Cut out two pieces of cardboard – one with a hole in the centre for the front of the frame, and one without a hole for the back.

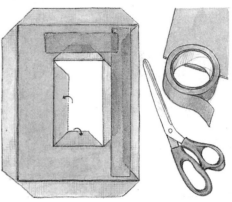

1. Trim the needlepoint, leaving 3cm/1¼" all around the edge. Cut diagonally across the corners and slit the centre as shown. Before folding, reinforce both the outer and inner canvas corners on the wrong side with a strong tape. Place the cardboard piece for the front of the frame over the back of the needlepoint. Fold the outer right-hand-side edge of the canvas over the frame and tape in place, leaving the remaining outer edges free. Fold over the inside edges and tape in place.

2. Place the cardboard piece for the back of the frame over the wrong side of the front piece. Fold the three remaining outer edges over the back of the frame and tape in place. Slide your photograph or drawing into place through the open edge.

ACKNOWLEDGEMENTS

First, acknowledgements to Steve Lovi, not only for the photography, but also for collaborating on the concepts of all of the projects in this book, as well as hunting down the exciting props and doing his inimitable styling throughout.

Like with most projects as elaborate as this, there has to be cooperation from many willing friends.

For hours of patient stitching, grateful thanks to Rory Mitchell, Barry McGinn, Kay Kettles, Elian McCready, Jill Gordon, Zoë Hunt and many helpful students. Thanks to Richard Womersley for not only putting up with the constant herd of helpers, but for providing us all with delicious sustenance.

Special thanks to the people who commissioned work and allowed it to be photographed: Mr and Mrs Collis (for the handsome blue orchard chair), Mr and Mrs Blackburn, Mr and Mrs Ehrman, Gay Leonhardt, Mr and Mrs Sachler and John Torson.

Particular thanks are due to those good friends who allowed us to photograph in their handsome houses or lent props: Antoinette Allsopp, Sandy Boler, Robert Buys, Susan Collier, John and Camilla Fairbairn, Polly and Andy Garnett, Tricia Guild, Pam Harlech, Bridget Keenan, Muriel Latow, Philippa Scott, June Henry and Anouska Weinberg.

Thanks to the Gallery of Antique Costume and Textiles for the loan of fabrics, to Putnams of Mill Lane for the loan of jugs and fabrics, and to Peter Adler for the loan of objects from his collection of primitive art. Steve would like to thank Pulbrook and Gould for being so helpful with flowers.

It is time here to thank Gail Rebuck for her generous belief in Steve and myself, when we had no track record in this publishing lark.

Thanks to Sally Harding for her conscientious hard work and her imaginative editing, to Serena Jones for her infinite attention to detail, and to Cherriwyn Magill for her classic style and for interpreting our brief so creatively.

Thank you to the Victoria and Albert Museum for inspiration, and to my faithful companion while working – Radio 4.

Lastly, a long-overdue thank you to Hugh Ehrman and Stephen Sheard for their enthusiastic support over the years.

YARN AND KIT INFORMATION

The needlepoint designs in this book list the specific types and colours of yarn to be used for a particular colourway illustrated. These are all Appleton or Rowan yarns and can be obtained either from yarn shops in the usual way or in the form of kits specially made up for some of the designs.

KITS AVAILABLE

The following designs are available as kits:

Kits	Page
1. Apple Cushion	14–15
2. Baroda Stripe	150
3. Blue-and-White Bowl Cushion	122–3
4. Cabbage Cushion	27
5. Carpet Bag	130
6. Carpet Garden	150
7. Cauliflower Cushion	27
8. Cherry Cushion	19
9. Delft Table Mat	60–1
10. Flower Pyramid Cushion	67
11. Flower Shoulder Bag	75
12. Flower Trellis Carpet	56
13. Flower Trellis Cushion	58–9
14. Fresco Star	151
15. Harvest Bowl	150
16. Leafy	150
17. Medallion Cushion	146–7
18. Night Tree	150
19. Oriental Fish Cushion	47
20. Paisley	150
21. Pear Cushion	14–15
22. Peony Jar	150
23. Plum Cushion	19
24. Sea Bird	150
25. Star Tile	151

ADDRESSES FOR KITS

For details of stockists and mail order sources of yarns and kits, please write to the following addresses:

UK and Europe

Rowan Yarns (stockists), Green Lane Mill, Holmfirth, West Yorkshire HD7 1RW, England. *Tel.* (0484) 686 714/687 374

Ehrman (mail order), 21/22 Vicarage Gate, London W8 4AA, England. *Tel.* (01) 937 4568

USA

Ehrman, 5 Northern Boulevard, Amherst, New Hampshire 03031. *Tel.* (603) 886 5054

Canada

Estelle, 38 Continental Place, Scarborough, Ontario M1R 2T4. *Tel.* (416) 298 9922

New Zealand

R. G. & P. A. Hoddinott, PO Box 1486, Auckland.

Australia

Sunspun, 195 Canterbury Road, Canterbury, Victoria 3126. *Tel.* (03) 830 1609

ADDRESSES FOR YARNS
UK and Europe

Appleton yarns are available from all leading needlepoint stockists in the UK. Listed below are some of the main needlework centres. But, if you have any difficulty in obtaining the yarns, please contact Appleton Bros Ltd at: Thames Works, Church Street, Chiswick, London W4 2PE (*Tel.* 01 994 0711).

Voirrey Embroidery Centre, Brimstage Hall, Brimstage, Wirrall L63 6JA. *Tel.* (051) 342 3514

Campden Needlecraft Centre, High Street, Chipping Campden, Gloucestershire. *Tel.* (0386) 840 583

Royal School of Needlework, 5 King Street, Covent Garden, London WC2 8HN. *Tel.* (01) 836 1108

Women's Home Industries Ltd, Tapestry Shop, 85 Pimlico Road, London SW1. *Tel.* (01) 730 5366

OSA, 2 The Parade, St Mary's Place, Shrewsbury, Shropshire. *Tel.* (074) 355 533

USA

American Crewel & Canvas Studio (wholesale distributors – please contact with any queries about obtaining Appleton yarns), PO Box 453, 164 Canal Street, Canastota, NY 13032, New York. *Tel.* (315) 697 3759

Elegant Needle Ltd, 5430 MacArthur Boulevard, Washington.

LASS Needlework Studio, 3000 E. Second Street, Long Beach, Calif.

Natalie, 144 N. Larchmont Boulevard, Los Angeles, Calif.

Needle Works Ltd, 4041 Tulane Avenue, New Orleans, LA.

Sign of the Arrow, St Louis, Mo.

Richard R. Trexler, 9509 Lawndale Avenue, Evanston, Ill.

Textile Museum Shop, 2320 S. Street NW, Washington D.C. 20008.

Australia

Clifton H. Joseph & Son, 391/393 Little Lonsdale Street, Melbourne.

Canada

Jet Handcraft Studio Ltd, 1836 Marine Drive, W. Vancouver.

One Stitch at a Time, Box 114, Picton, Ontario.

New Zealand

Nancy's Embroidery Ltd, c/o James Smith Ltd, Cuba Street, Wellington.

INDEX

Page numbers in *italic* refer to instructions.

Apple cushion 15, 16
Autumn landscape tapestry 11, 84–5

Backgrounds 10
Backings 128
Bags, carpet *130–2*; flower *74–5*; handles 157; lobster *38–41*; straps 74, 130; striped knitting *132*, *135–6*,157
Bargello flower bench 78–9
Baroda stripe cushion 150–1
Blocking 11, 155
Blue-and-white pot cushion *119–24*
Blue orchard chair 10, *28–31*
Borders 128
Bouquet cushion *68–71*
Buddha cushion *102–5*, 108

Cabbage, cushion *24*; placemat *21*, *27*
Canvas, gauge 7, 152; linen 152; preparing 155; tinting 58, 155; transferring design onto 11, 36, 154; types of 152
Carpet bag *130–2*
Carpet garden cushion 150–1
Carpets and rugs, flower trellis 27, 54–8; yellow rug 143–5
Cats 99–102
Caucasian flower cushion 84, 86
Cauliflower, cushion *24;* placemat *24*, *27*
Chairs 10, 11
   blue orchard *28–31;* tropical floral 80–1, 83
Charts, working from 154–5
Child's head cushion 107–10
China pot tapestry 126–7
Cleaning needlepoint 156
Colour 10, 64, 152
   animation achieved by 8–9; black and white 34; blue and white 58, 62, 110, 119–21; matching 6, 11, 152; mixing from crewel threads 11, 41, 96, 100, 108, 154; shading 154; tone 11, 34, 154
Cosmos tapestry 7, 138–9
Cushions, apple 15, 16; backing 156; baroda stripe 150–1; blue-and-white pot *119–24*; bouquet *68–71*; Buddha *102–5*, *108*; cabbage *24*; carpet garden 150–1; caucasian flower 84, 86; cauliflower *24;* child's head 107–10; duck *47–9*; edges 10; flower pyramid *64–8*; flower trellis *57–8*; fresco star 151; Harvest Bowl 150–1;

jug-shaped 119–20; Kabuki face *91*, *92*, *94–6*, 154, 157; kits 150–1, 158; Leafy 150–1; medallion *146–8*; mitred frame 157; Night Tree 150–1; oriental fish 46–7; Paisley 150–1; pear *16–18*; Peony Jar 150–1; pheasant 46; piping 158; plaid *126*, *128–30*; plum *12*, *16–19*; rooster 46; ruffles 156–7; Sea Bird 150–1; shaped 47–9, 102, 108, 119, 120; Star Tile 151

Delft table mat *58*, *61–4*
Designing 6, 8–11, 154
Design sources 9–10, 28, 30
   eggs 32, 52; faces and fans 89–117; fish and fowl 32–53; flowers and foliage 54–87; fruits and vegetables 12–31; jugs and geometrics 119–49; lichens 8, 140, 143, 157; marquetry 65, 73; shells 9, 10, 32–6, 41; translating into needlepoint 10–11
Duck cushions *47–9*

Egg pot holder 52

Fan, lampshade 94, 116; throw 54, 112, 114, 116
Flower pyramid cushion *64–8*
Flower shoulder bag *74–7*
Flower trellis carpet and cushion 27, *54–8*
Frames, for embroidery 11, 57, 155; mitred frame for cushion 157; picture *140*, *143*, 157
Fresco Star cushion 151

Garden tapestry bench 6, 82–4

Handles 157
Harvest Bowl tapestry 8, 150–1
Headboards 41
Heritage tapestry 7–8, 100–1

Joint projects 7–8, 100–1, 138–9
Jug-shaped cushions 119–20

Kabuki face cushion *91*, *92*, *94–6*, 154, 157
Kits 9, 150–1
   list of 158

Lampshades, fan 94, 116; marble cone shell motif *34*, *36–7*; scallop shell 32, 34
Leafy design 150–1
Lichen picture frame 8, *140*, *143*, 157
Lobster bag 38–41

Marble cone shell motif *34*, *36–7*
Medallion cushion *146–8*

Mosaic head 7, 110–11, 114

Needles 153
Night Tree cushion 150–1

Oriental arrangement tapestry 9, 119
Oriental fish cushion 46–7

Paisley cushion 150–1
Paperweight 7
Pear cushion *16–18*
Peony Jar 150–1
Petit-point 152
Pheasant cushion 46
Piping 156
Plaids, borders 128: backings 30, 128; cushions *126*, *128–30*
Plum cushion 12, *16–19*

Repeating patterns 7, 74
Rooster, cushion 46; tea cosy *43–6*
Ruffles 156–7
Rugs *see* Carpets and rugs

Sea Bird cushion 150–1
Seams 155–6
Shell, bedcover 10; headboard 41; lampshade *32*, *34*
Sizing 155
Sketching 28
Slippers 6
Spectacles case *143–6*
Star Tile cushion 151
Stitches, basktweave tent 153; continental tent 153; direction of 78; half cross 152–3, 155–6; leaving out 94; seams 155–6; random long 7, 8, 115, 153–4; tent 6, 8, 153
Stone head 96–7, 100
Striped knitting bag *132*, *135–6*, 157

Table mats, cabbage and cauliflower 21, *24*, *27*; Delft *58*, *61–4*
Tapestries, autumn landscape 11, 84–5; blending with old 82–4; china pot 126–7; Cosmos 7, 138–9; garden tapestry bench 6, 82–4; Heritage 7–8, 100–1; oriental arrangement 9, 119; tulip 73, 74
Tea cosy *43–6*
Techniques 152–7
Templates 11, 36, 92, 155
Transferring a design 11, 36, 154
Tropical floral chair 80–1, 83
Tulip tapestry 73, 74

Yarn, crewel 11, 41, 96, 100, 108, 152, 154; dye lots 152; length 153; Persian 152; tapestry 152
Yellow rug 143–5

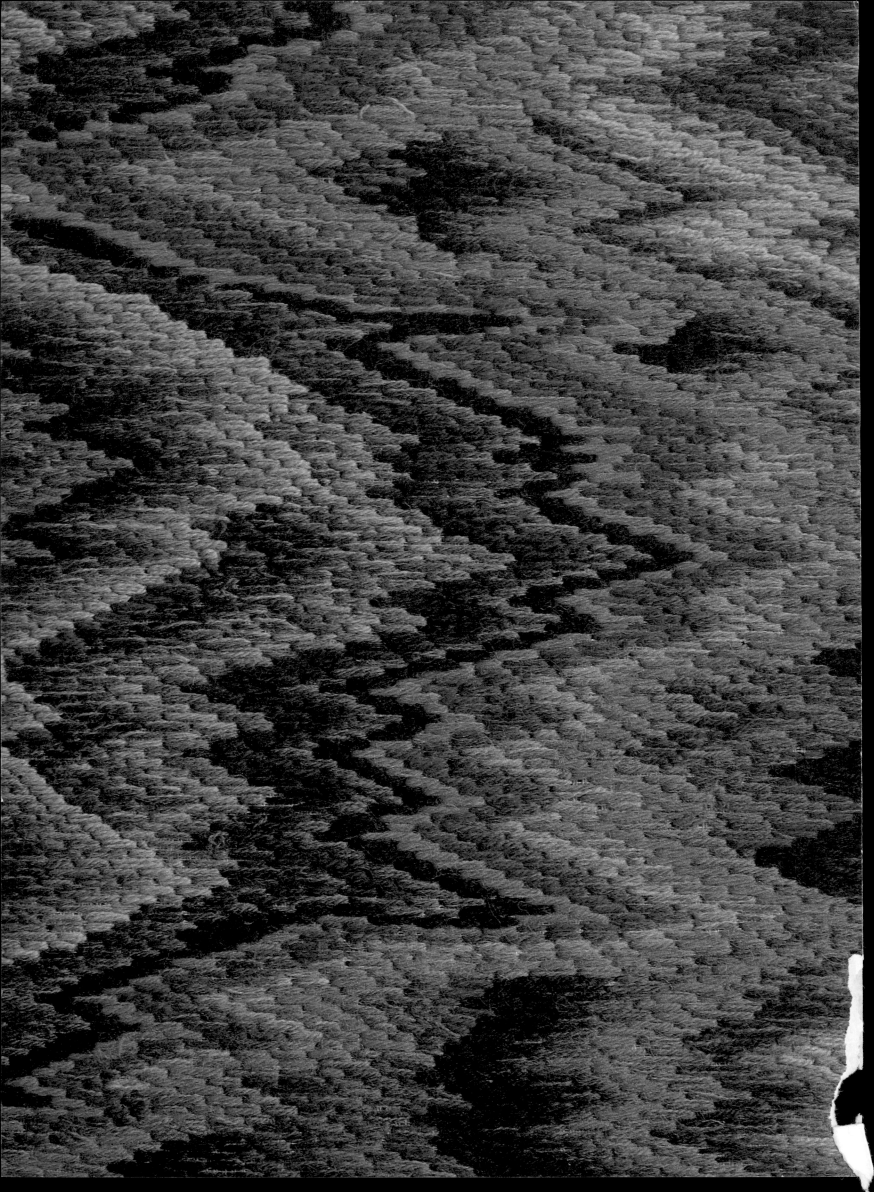